What I Do

(Memoirs)

If it is your life
A Lean Third
That Was a Shiver

<u>Drama</u>

Hardie and Baird & other plays

<u>Essays</u>

Some Recent Attacks: Essays Cultural & Political
"And the judges said . . ."

What I do

(Memoirs)

JAMES KELMAN

thi-wurd.com

First published in Glasgow, Scotland in 2020 by thi wurd

This edition first published in this format 2020 by thi wurd

Book only ISBN 978-1-8381030-0-2
eBook ISBN 978-1-8381030-1-9

British Library Cataloguing-in-Publication Data
A catalogue record for this book is available from the British Library

Cover design by Andrew Cattanach
Designed and typeset by Biblichor Ltd, Edinburgh
Printed and bound by Clays Ltd, Elcograf S.p.A.

The writings collected here were written firstly to be read or heard whether as obituary, memorial or eulogy. Most have been revised, and some thoroughly. I never met Harry McShane, Alex La Guma or Amos Tutuola personally, but each of the others I considered a friend.

for
Sarah White and Roxy Harris

Contents

What I do is Write[1]

Mary Gray Hughes was a great friend to me when I was a young writer. We met at the home of her friends, Anne Stevenson and Philip Hobsbaum, who were both poets. Anne was the daughter of the philosopher Charles L. Stevenson and she and Mary Gray had been friends since their student days. Philip was a professor in the English Department at the University of Glasgow and ran a weekly night class on Creative Writing for the Extra-Mural department. I was driving buses for a living, on shift work, and attended when I could, usually on alternate weeks.

This was the spring of 1972 in Glasgow, Scotland and Mary Gray was the main guest of the evening. Others had been invited along to meet the visiting writer but they barely got a look in: I hogged her company. I recollect not so much the conversation but my enjoyment of it: the talk would have been of art, in particular literature, the lives of artists and writers. I remember that we managed to keep our same seats for most of the evening; that would have been a two to three hour period, amazing – I don't think I even visited the bathroom, probably scared somebody would steal her away. I was twenty-five years of age, Mary Gray closer to forty.

What I Do

More than twenty years passed until our next meeting which was in a hotel lobby in Chicago in 1995 but we had corresponded. The first letter she sent me is dated June 1972, the time she was finishing a fine story of hers entitled *The Calling*, about an idealistic young minister. We remained in touch, two or three letters a year, sometimes more, depending on the situation. Following the death of her husband, John, in 1992, her letters became fewer, and irregular.

Writers need contact with one another. I was only then beginning to meet people with whom I could communicate. Most of the time I drove buses for a living and my wife Marie also worked, part-time then full-time; soon she became the major breadwinner. I had made the decision to become a full-time writer one way or another and she was with me all the way. When not in paid employment I wrote non-stop, between breaks looking after the children. A writer was a writer, gender was relevant but only slightly. The long-distance conversation with Mary Gray was crucial; me in Glasgow, she in Evanston, Illinois. We shared the usual preoccupations of adult artists: domestic economics, how to contribute to the household coffers. My own opinion is that where possible it is better that artists lead lives of ordinary, everyday commitment, and I wanted to be a proper parent. And one thing about being a parent, it can keep you from contemplating too seriously "a long swim in the cold, polluted Lake Michigan." She spoke of her family in her letters. One of her daughters, Margaret Henderson, remembers the day her mother sold a short story to a magazine. "I must have been six or eight . . . We all were very excited and danced in a circle . . . She spent a huge amount of time with her children. I don't think any of us felt her writing made her less of a mother; it made her more of a mother."

The powerful, poignant title story of Mary Gray's first collection, The Thousand Springs, is the briefest of diary extracts in the life of a woman whose passion is literature and who strives to write and to find sufficient space in the drudgery of everyday existence. In spite of all, she does manage to steal fifteen minutes "each night. At the table." I use this story for students on Creative Writing courses, when I discuss the absurdity of the 'blank page'. Necessity is relative and for many writers and would-be writers, especially women, the mixture of domestic and necessity is crippling. Far too many of those writers are 'silenced', a subject upon which her friend Tillie Olsen published the seminal work, Silences.

Mary Gray had suggested I seek an arts council grant. Eventually I did, and was awarded the sum of £500, not a lot of money even in those days. Nevertheless £400 of it became the deposit towards a two-bedroom apartment. She predicted that sometime in the future I would be able to do a little teaching, even though I had no university qualifications, my publications would suffice. This proved to be the case and throughout the years I have been able to earn a bit of occasional money by "teaching Creative Writing". Like Mary Gray herself, who for several years taught on a part-time basis at Northeastern University, Illinois where her husband was based. She was of the opinion that you cannot teach writing. I don't so much disagree as look on the matter differently. I wish we had had the chance to talk it out, I suspect our disagreement may have derived from a misunderstanding.

As early as 1972 she referred to having begun work on "something longer" and I believe this was an early stab at the story that would become her only novel, The Empty Lot. During the years I mentioned the "long thing" to her but she was not forthcoming. One comment she made stuck with me, said in reference to her writing generally: "everything I touch turns to ashes." It was not until 1992, finally, that her novel was published. But the physical and enduring trauma she suffered from a road traffic accident twenty years earlier cannot be forgotten here.

Mary Gray had no time for 'frauds' and she thought that "the trouble over here [in USA] is the quantity of people, in writing and everything else, who . . . write and read for money or fame or this and that, and too rarely because of writing itself." The things she was saying in her letters were what all young artists need to hear. "Don't let the success of the second and third rate get you down, they never last." "The literary hacks can't harm your writing, only you can do that." "The lives of most writers are one thing, the work another."

She had already shown a batch of my stories to her close friend and first publisher, the poet Constance Hunting, founder of Puckerbrush Press. That was the summer of 1972 and she sent a handful of my early stories to her agent Pat Myrer in New

York City. Of course she made sure I would keep my feet on the ground, not to expect to make any money out of it. I was just glad of the attention, glad to be taken seriously, especially by a writer whose integrity of purpose, whose love of literary art was clear from our first meeting. Her first collection of stories, The Thousand Springs, had been published in 1971 and here she was only one year later assisting a young writer to come forward. A further lesson here for the young writer, concerning generosity, how an artist should behave to other artists.

She offered a critique on a few of my stories; in the early days she advised caution in my use of 'dialect', warning me of the risk of alienating the reader. She recommended that I look at the work of Flannery O'Connor and Emily Dickinson, and consider also Emily Brontë's use of 'dialect' in Wuthering Heights. Of course I had my own opinions and in reply I sent her another of my own stories, this time written in a first-person narrative and using a phonetic transcription, trying to capture the rhythms of an ordinary Glaswegian speaking voice. A short time later Mary Gray wrote, "Forget all I said about dialect . . . you obviously know what you are doing better than anyone."

Her story *The Judge* had just been taken for an anthology; it was typical of her not to mention the title of "the anthology": The Best American Short Stories 1972. What a marvellous story *The Judge* is, the lives of these two elderly men and that sense of place, that great feel of Texas. Although she lived most of her adult life in the northern states Mary Gray hailed from

Brownsville, the southernmost town in the entire country. Perhaps her girlhood experiences of being raised in a border town aided her sensitivity to questions relating to race and class, to social veneers. In *The Judge* these preoccupations are realized gloriously in the 'friendship' that disguises a relationship grounded on power between the judge and the Mexican small-holder. Many American people know little about the so-called third world. Down along the Mexican border people just have to cross the bridge, even before you reach the other side the difference can be acute.

I looked forward to her correspondence very much. There came a period when no letters arrived, not for a long time. I heard the upsetting news from Philip Hobsbaum that Mary Gray had been involved in

a terrible automobile accident . . . It is a miracle she is alive. John [her husband] was also injured but not so badly. A van jumped the median, crossed two lanes on Chicago's outer drive by the lakes and hit them head on. [Mary Gray] sustained multiple injuries both external and internal . . .

In April she was still in hospital, "only lately recovered enough to write anything." Each of her hands and wrists had been "strapped to boards" and she was "unable to focus . . . irrational, or just not there, for a long time . . . and it seems it's a slow process to come back from wherever one goes when one's not there . . ."

Something I wrote to her then embarrassed me later; I spoke of how I could envy people's direct experiences, even things like terrible car accidents. In mitigation, I was only twenty-six at the time. Mary Gray let me off the hook, "so many writers want to experience everything – even war." She said she was taking "pages of notes on hospital life . . . strange world, based on . . . sadness and suffering."

The severity of this accident had an unquestionable effect on her work. In a letter dated 25 November, 1974 it was "getting on for two years since the accident" and she had experienced many "ups and downs on the recovery route" but was hoping "to go on mending." A month after that letter was "a red letter day"; Mary Gray finished her first new story since before the accident. Even so her stories were a long time in the writing, "more than the usual slowness."

Eventually she was reading, and rereading, all the novels of Willa Cather, the stories of Dorothy Porter, a couple of which she thought "first-rate". And Kate Chopin, Doris Lessing, Isak Dinesen, and Correspondences, a new work by her friend Anne Stevenson. She enjoyed a tape of Katherine Ann Porter reading her own stories, and commented on a tape she had of Flannery O'Connor reading *A Good Man is Hard to Find* that reveals just "how funny [O'Connor] thought it was." Meanwhile she anticipated keenly the publication of Yonnondio, Tillie Olsen's one and only novel, most of which was written forty years earlier.

It was through Mary Gray I got to know Olsen's work. Her story *Tell Me a Riddle* is one of the great pieces of twentieth century American art. When Americans use the term "American" it is to describe a being with greater humanity than non-Americans. This is indicated constantly and clearly to the remainder of humankind when we hear statements such as "The suspected terrorist was charged with attempting to murder Americans." Not just ordinary people but Americans, it is hard even to call them people, they are better than that. Americans are just – my God, give me that guy's autograph he is an American; The Church Of The Latter Day Americans – it is hard not to be facetious.

The story *Tell Me a Riddle* offers a challenge to this aspect of American society that, even to a friendly alien, only seems to survive on a strange form of collective *mauvaise foi*, what the existentialists call 'bad faith'. This is a story about the 'secret history of the USA', it is about roots, about assimilation and its inherent dangers, and a truth too often denied, abused or simply unacknowledged, that the entire population, apart from its Native Americans, are either refugees, slaves, or from refugee or slave stock. It is not a story to bring comfort to those who are blind to the effects of so-called globalisation, of US hegemony.

There is never a good time for constructive criticism, especially in politics and especially from 'one of your own'; witness the establishment's attack on those who do not take the coward's way out, those who refuse to toe the line, whether physically or intellectually.

Little if any art worthy of the name is ever created in compromise which is why political authorities and society's leaders and elite groupings everywhere are so suspicious of it. Nowadays, with the degeneration of the book industry, the writers who do not compromise do not 'get sold', not properly. And distinguish between 'get sold' and 'sell'. Writers are happy to take their chances of selling to the public, assuming their work is in front of the public. The problem is that the book industry is selective about the literature it puts in front of the public. The art created by good US artists cannot push a comfortable view of American society. It would be a contradiction.

Mary Gray sent me a copy of the first Delacorte Press paperback edition of Olsen's stories, probably her own copy. She had the habit of giving away her favourite books. Also around that time Flannery O'Connor's complete stories had just been published in hardback. A friend had been over in New York for a few days staying with my brother and brought me back a copy as a present. Mary Gray thought O'Connor's work was "a great education in how to stick to one's own talent, never be tempted off it, and so get bigger by getting deeper."

There was cheering news on the road to recovery: the Southwest Review had taken another of her stories which meant she had just one left unpublished in the entire world! "Well, no, say 100." But that unpublished one was the only thing fit to be seen, in her opinion. I reckon the one referred to was *The Rock Garden*, which appeared in the spring 1973 edition of Southwest Review.

Some stories make more sense as I become older. When I last read *The Rock Garden* it was in light of the contemporary political situation, since the destruction of the Twin Towers in New York. The values of the female central character seem so acutely American, or should I say Anglo-American. For friendly aliens like myself it can be excruciating to behold. As the story progresses it becomes clear that the woman is descending into her own private world, one bound by an advancing dementia, perhaps Alzheimer's disease.

Mary Gray had the utmost respect, and affection, for the literary 'little' magazine and small press tradition, urging me never to underestimate their importance for 'real writers', citing its value for Flannery O'Connor and another great Texan writer, Katherine Ann Porter. I had good cause to appreciate that. In 1992, after a gap of twenty years since the first edition, Puckerbrush Press published the second edition of An Old Pub Near the Angel and it was twice reprinted after that. On the small press scene that represents a best-seller. Although I received ten copies of the new edition I never did receive any money.

Whenever Constance Hunting earned anything it was ploughed into new publications, mainly by local writers and poets from the area around Maine. I felt privileged to be part of it, as would any young writer. I never met Constance personally. I wish I had. She and Mary Gray were long-standing friends and tried to see each other whenever possible. Constance kept in touch with her writers and got a kick out of seeing us move on. She died in early 2006 at the age of seventy-nine. She was one of the great literary figures in that small press tradition and it was an honour for me to dedicate the first Scottish publication of An Old Pub Near the Angel to her memory, twenty five years after the first Puckerbrush edition.

The Southwest Review was Texas-based and perhaps Mary Gray favoured it for that reason. She always referred to it warmly in her letters. In those days for fiction they paid something like half a cent a word. Half a cent a word? "Oh yeh," she said, "but my God, so what! If you want to earn money don't be a writer, at least not a 'real writer', go do something else, try picking up dropped pennies in movie houses." Always be aware, that "writing has a lot of grimness in it."

In one letter she spoke of her plans to make a trip home on family business but along the way she planned a west Texas detour, as far as Odessa, where the Southwest Review was published. She wanted to meet up with the folk who ran it. With their sort of generosity and love of contemporary literature they were to be treasured.

Following that long stay in hospital after the accident she was allowed home, eventually, on crutches, her left leg in a brace; and so it remained for several months. There were problems too with her eyesight. But she was so glad to be home with her husband and children, where she could "breathe again." It was almost two years after the accident before she felt herself definitely "mending . . . getting a lot more energy . . . at least free of all the people I had to have last year to manage the house and that sort of thing . . ." She was managing to do some of her own work now, her writing.

This was 1975 and her father died in May of that year in Austin, Texas. Her father was Hart Stilwell, a well-known journalist and author, especially in his home state, "with a reputation as a maverick political commentator."[2] Her mother was Anne Gray Seabury, a social worker who on one occasion "helped [Stilwell] write a book on neglected children." Mary Gray later sent me her father's novel, Uncovered Wagon, which I read once and thought it was great, and loaned it to somebody immediately. And that was the last ever I saw it. Later I managed to acquire another copy.

Stilwell's writings were "marked by a fierce liberalism and hatred of intolerance."[3] He was born in Yoakum, a few miles east of San Antonio and graduated from the University of Texas at Austin (UT Austin). He was an acquaintance and correspondent of the legendary J. Frank Dobie. Another of Dobie's correspondents was the Scottish writer, traveller, political radical and fine horseman, R. B. Cunninghame Graham, who owned for a period a ranch in the San Antonio area. Some of the letters of Dobie and Cunninghame Graham can be found at the Harry Ransome Centre.

Cunninghame Graham was a character who would have appealed greatly to Mary Gray. Another prolific writer, his correspondents included George Bernard Shaw, Keir Hardie, Peter Kropotkin and James Connolly. The Texas School of Writers is now known as The Michener Centre and based literally in J. Frank Dobie's old house on the edge of the UT campus in Austin. Many writers will carry strong memories of it for the rest of their lives. Back in the 1920s Hart Stilwell was one, talking away the night in that fine old house with the burn flowing at the foot of the back garden. I also have good memories of the house, from when I taught three semesters at UT Austin (1999–2002).

Mary Gray described her father's Uncovered Wagon as "an 'autobiography'" and said that "[he] changed names and place names" because his own mother "objected to the harshness of his narrative." Stilwell's own "upbringing [had been] marked by psychological and physical conflict with his father, a former Texas Ranger prone to sudden mood swings and threats of violence."[4] The novel "included a thinly fictionalized account of his relationship with his father, called 'The Old Man' in the book [and] was named one of the fifty best books of Texas by A. C. Greene, who wrote 'you don't find many Texas writers who can face the bitter reality of rural poverty in a changing society as Stilwell does.'"[5]

Such 'bitter reality' formed a crucial part of the base material of Mary Gray's own stories, including some of her best work. But her preoccupations also leaned to the ease with which human beings may be edged, often by their own machinations, into existential space, into waking nightmares, or into simply becoming deranged, entering into dementia or madness itself.

Stilwell worked for a short period as a full-time newspaper-man but he gave it up while still in his twenties and turned to making his living freelance. Unless you get a stroke of amazing fortune, living as a full-time writer is another way of living on your wits. Where possible you are prepared to turn your hand to any writing 'chore' if and when requested. Of course it is not always possible. Some of these 'chores' ask a little too much of a writer, one compromise too many. So there is a line the 'working' writer has to walk. None I ever met underestimates the problem. Mary Gray was very conscious of the fact. Never more than when following the death of her father she

> went down to Texas. Sat at his desk. Covered with rejection slips, a few acceptances, lists of places he was sending or would send articles and stories and a book. A lifelong writer, successful, never giving in, never quitting, and simply taking rejection slips as part of the trade. No matter what, never quitting. Superb.

A month later – and surely no coincidence – she "finished a new story . . . the first new thing since the damned accident [and was] now working on two other stories, in my usual pretty slow way." Looking back on this period through her letters I get an idea of the massive effect the "damned accident" had on her writing life. She also wanted to work on her "longer thing" but could not fight her way in properly, she needed more practice before tackling an extended work. A few months on from then she was "polishing off . . . [a] new story . . . in stride again, and doing pretty much what I want," reading stories by

George Mackay Brown ["nice steady writer"] from the Orkney islands.

The second and only other occasion we were ever to meet, after a gap of twenty-three years, was in Chicago, 1995. Following the publication of my novel How Late It Was, How Late, I was passing through in the middle of a reading tour. It was hectic. Mary Gray also had commitments. Eventually we spent two hours chatting over coffee in a hotel lobby. It was an awkward meeting. There was too much there for me, perhaps not for her, being the older writer, too much I needed to say and did not or could not. When she left to return home I felt a sadness. She walked by herself to the door and I stayed where I was. It was a strange moment. There were things I wanted to say. Who knows what I did say, I cannot remember. I was aware that this was our only meeting since that first occasion back in 1972 and I didn't expect we would meet again; it was not in any way momentous, except being there in her presence, it was just quiet, sitting there in that hotel lobby.

There was nothing more. I wished I could have expressed things to her. I didn't. The dedications I gave to her did not do justice to her generosity.

When I was teaching at UT Austin I was disappointed to discover that her work was virtually unknown there. But her output only amounted to one novel, two slim volumes of short stories and much uncollected poetry, so although disappointed by the lack of recognition in her home state I was far from astonished. I cannot remember a single American student from

my short periods teaching in Austin then in San José, California who had heard of Tillie Olsen or June Jordan either. It
would have pleased Mary Gray to know that her archive is now
resting in the Southwestern Writers Collection, Texas State
University, San Marcos.

I remember in 1975 I had given up driving buses and was
working in a factory, alternate fortnights of day and night
shift. Marie was working too and our girls were four and five
years old. It was difficult, and the inherent frustrations for
myself, not being able to write and so on, yes, it drove me
crazy. And Marie had to live it with me, so it was a bad time.
In a letter to Mary Gray I discussed some of that and how I felt
that I could "see clearly when . . . depressed, and not writing."
The earlier quote about Lake Michigan was from Mary Gray
so she knew the feeling alright but wondered perhaps if it was
not closer to

> the near madness of that state. I know I feel that I am seeing
> into the centre of the earth, seeing the truth, and am dead
> right. Afterwards, that black vision strikes me as simply
> deranged. Yet it's that derangement one uses, somewhere, in
> one's work.
>
> Or I do. No matter. No matter even understanding it.
> What I do is write. And the best fun, sometimes, is in the
> writing. In getting a few words, even one word, right. Or a
> whole story right. There's truth in that feeling, too. It's not
> just the gloomy views that are the true ones.

Her commitment to literature was close to total, given she was married and had three children. In my own case it was through Mary Gray that my first collection of stories appeared. I am not overstating the case to describe Mary Gray Hughes as one of the most crucial people in my life. At that critical period no one's influence was more significant. It was a pleasure to know that Constance Hunting had gathered enough new stories for a posthumous collection and an honour to be asked to contribute this introduction.

Calum and the Print Studio Press

The Glasgow Print Studio did not have 'a press' nor any printing operation. What they had was a wonderful facilitator, Calum Mackenzie, who gave people the opportunity to go there and do stuff for themselves. Out of that a few writers worked together to produce a series of pamphlets. We met at the Print Studio, and a couple of pubs. In discussion with Calum we named ourselves the Print Studio Press. Without Calum there would have been no Print Studio Press.

In those days it was based in Ingram Street, having flitted very recently from St Vincent Crescent. Here is my own brief recollection of that. Others may see it differently.

I had begun at the University of Strathclyde in October 1975 at the age of twenty-nine. What a relief to escape bus driving and factory work. I saw unlimited writing time ahead for the next three to four years. I had all these damn stories and projects on the go. All I had to do was conform to certain criteria, the most important of which was completing the written work and passing exams.

In those days there was what was known as 'the mature student's grant'. This was earnings related and based upon the wages earned during the previous three or five years. It was brought in by a Labour Government and was designed to give older working class people the chance to go through higher education, especially those of us with family commitments. The 'earnings related grant' gave us a chance. It meant we weren't dropping too much income. But it was still very basic. Even with my wife Marie's part-time earnings it still was not enough. I needed part-time work myself. Occasionally I served behind the bar in the old Pewter Pot, in those days located at the corner of South and North Woodside Road. I lived closeby. So did Calum. In those days the Pewter Pot was a popular haunt of writers, actors, BBC employees and various artists, including John Taylor, Jackie Parry and Calum Mackenzie. This is how I got to know the Print Studio Gallery.

I found university difficult. If I made it there in the morning I was defeated by lunchtime. Luckily the Print Studio had by now moved to Ingram Street from Finnieston and writers were welcomed along. It was an adventurous space run mainly by Calum, supported strongly by the gallery's administrator Catriona Clark, Johnnie Taylor, Jackie Parry and others. But it was Calum in charge and he who offered the space, the freedom, the facilities.

He was keen on interdisciplinary work among artists. While based in St Vincent Crescent he encouraged joint projects with Liz Lochhead, Tom Leonard and Aonghas Macneacail. Writers were further encouraged to organise readings, and to be involved generally. Through his enthusiasm the Print Studio staged John Byrne's first play, Writer's Cramp, during that same period.

Also Calum was a collector of rare Scottish books. I remember he had a very early edition of Martin Martin's A Description of the Western Islands of Scotland, and the first edition of J. F. Campbell's Popular Tales of the West Highlands. The Print Studio became a sanctuary for myself.

By 1977 some of us writers thought to form the Print Studio Press, as a cooperative. I stress this was a cooperative among writers. The Print Studio did not publish us. We published ourselves. We set to produce our own good quality pamphlets (mainly work that nobody else would publish). Within a short period of time, aside from my Short Tales from the Nightshift, we produced Forwords by Tom Buchan and Islands by Liz Lochhead. Tom Buchan actually published his one himself, the first in the series, but appreciated being part of it. My collection, Short Tales from the Nightshift, followed, with artwork by Maggie Wallace.

Our original intention was to do it all ourselves, and have proper artists from the Print Studio network engage on the graphics. Between us we had ample experience to organise and accomplish this. Calum had great news one day, through one of his many contacts he was in a position to acquire sundry casefuls of lead type at genyoooine knock-down prices. Calum accomplished these acquisitional chores with a grin, a wink and a nudge-nudge of the elbow. I was more excited than him, given my experience as a boy compositor. I served more than two years as an apprentice. Thus I thought myself equipped to give it a go setting the books by hand. Liz Lochhead and Alan Spence volunteered to assist me. (What faith!) Then we would print the books ourselves. Jim Taylor, the Scottish-Australian poet and publisher was then domiciled in Glasgow. He volunteered to take a lead role in the printing.

But one thing soon became clear: doing everything ourselves was a pipe-dream. We needed a proper printer and needed to raise the dough ourselves. Nobody got money from Calum, apart from Catriona who somehow kept things afloat.

There were mad fundraising nights. One happened at a wee gallery directed by Richard Demarco. It was scheduled for midnight. Two auld guys and a dug turned up. Just as well. We had spent the evening in that bar in Stewart Street where we managed to talk ourselves out of a fight. We were guilty of laughing too loudly. We did other readings in the Print Studio itself, and plenty other stuff. Thus we were able to pay Heatherbank Press of Milngavie to print and produce the work professionally. But us writers took responsibility for the layout of our own books, the graphics and so on, aside from the Print Studio Press logo which was created by Alasdair Gray.

Once we had published the first two books the Scottish Arts Council allocated fifty quid towards the next, and on a book by book basis thereafter. Tom Buchan's Forwords was first and my Short Tales from the Nightshift second, then Tom Leonard's brilliant If Only Bunty Was Here, a drama written for radio. We produced Muthos for Logos by Jim Taylor; The Comedy of the White Dog by Alasdair Gray; Glasgow Zen by Alan Spence; The One-legged Tapdancer by Carl MacDougall and Imaginary Wounds by Aonghas Macneacail. We were to be doing further titles by Tom McGrath and Brian McCabe but by then the operation had petered out.

It only came into existence through the energy and commitment of the writers. We were never a 'publisher', we were a cooperative; and once a cooperative ends, that is that.

Nobody ever makes money from these cooperative ventures. The opposite is the case. The Scottish Arts Council came in with support and that was great. But the books cost us money to produce, as well as the time and effort. Those of us based in Glasgow were the chief working members. Alasdair was general secretary, minutes secretary and secretary of other stuff too. One of my own roles was treasurer. I conducted business very strictly: so strictly I still have the chequebook and payslips, plus the remaining £105 in the Bank of Ireland. At least as far as I know, I have not enquired since 1980. Calum and myself were going to invite Liz, Tom, Alasdair, Johnny T and other pals to help us drink it in the old Pewter Pot but the pub closed down in anticipation. Calum, Catriona, Tom Buchan, Tom Leonard and Alasdair Gray are no longer with us. I raise my glass to them: slàinte.

Why ain't the band playing?

'I'd like to sit down in a smart caffy one day and eat my way right out of a load of turkey, roast potatoes, beet salad and angel's food trifle. With port and cigars at the end.'

'Hell,' said Whitey, 'it's all a matter of taste. Some people like chicken and others eat sheep's head and beans.'

'A matter of taste,' Chinaboy scowled. 'Bull, it's a matter of money, pal. I worked six months in that caffy and I never heard nobody order sheep's head and beans!'

'You heard of the fellow who went into one of these big caffies?' Whitey asked, whirling the last of his coffee around in the tin cup. 'He sits down at a table and takes out a packet of sandwiches and puts it down. Then he calls the waiter and orders a glass of water. When the waiter brings the water, this fellow says: "Why ain't the band playing?"'

We chuckled over that and Chinaboy almost choked. He coughed and spluttered a little and then said, 'Another John goes into a caffy and orders sausage and mash. When the waiter brings him the stuff he take a look and say: "My dear

man, you've brought me a cracked plate." "Hell," says the
waiter. "That's no crack. That's the sausage."'

Above is an extract from a short story by Alex La Guma, a
South African writer who died of a heart attack in October
1985; he was sixty years of age and living in Havana, the African National Congress (ANC) representative in Cuba. This
was still a bleak period in the history of what is now the Repub-
lic of South Africa, yet chinks of light had appeared. The
anti-apartheid movement had gained strength.[1] There was
widespread revulsion at the barbarism of the fascist white
regime. Even so it survived for another eight years. It would not
have survived without the support of the British State, the US
State, the Israeli State. The usual tactic of condemning the
liberation forces at any opportunity was invoked. Its leading
formation, the ANC, was labelled a "terrorist organisation" by
none other than the British Prime Minister.

In that year of 1985 "the apartheid government's complete
clamp-down of citizens' rights resulted in numerous house
arrests of influential anti-apartheid leaders, and the detaining
of 2,346 people under the Internal Security Act."[2] Very many
thousands were in exile abroad, and had been for years. One
was Alex La Guma. I had known and respected his work for a
while, especially his early collection of short stories, A Walk in
the Night. One story in particular stuck with me, *A Matter of
Taste*, from which the opening quotation is taken. It is a marvellous bit of writing, telling of three men who meet over a pot of

coffee in the middle of nowhere. They have a meandering conversation centred on food, then the two help the third hop a freight train heading for Cape Town wherein lies the possibility of working a passage to the USA.

In the racial parlance of white South African authority the two are 'coloured', not 'black', and the third is 'white'. La Guma himself was 'coloured'. If the reader forgets such distinctions it won't be for long for it is always there, the backdrop to his work. And it cannot be extricated from it, nor from the deadly suffocating nature of that racist society. Even in that brief extract above the divisions are evident, where Whitey sees choice and Chinaboy knows differently.

The title story of the collection is the short novel, *A Walk in the Night*, which is really a very fine piece of writing. I did not appreciate this at the first time of reading. There was something missing for me which I see now as structural. In *A Matter of Taste* there was no missing element as such and my appreciation of the story was immediate. The situation reminded me of conversations between men on the edge, scraping by, no dough hardly at all and where most of the talk is on what is absent. Irony is central and irony was immediately present in *A Matter of Taste*.

Not so in *A Walk in the Night*, set in the 'coloured' District 6 which used to be one of the worst slums in Cape Town until it was done away with altogether to create space for white building development. In La Guma's story a young man by the name of Michael Adonis gets the sack after a verbal disagreement with a white man. For the rest of the evening he wanders about in a semi-daze, going for a meal, periodically meeting with acquaintances, would-be gangsters. In a moment of stupidity he vents his anger on an elderly white man, an Irish alcoholic who lives in the same rooming house. The old man dies.

Then the white policemen arrive and one of Michael's acquaintances winds up being mistaken for him, i.e. the killer. It is a memorable story, like most of the others in the collection. The structural element I spoke of as missing for me in my initial reading is to do with empathy; I found it very difficult to be with Michael Adonis, the world he moved in; it was alien to me. But I read the story again. It was less 'alien' on this second reading. The last time I read the story I knew this world even more. Not thoroughly, but enough to move along with Michael Adonis.

Speaking purely as a writer it is good to feel anything and everything is possible in experiential terms. The existence of apartheid made such a thing less easy to assume. In a good interview by Ian Fullerton and Glen Murray,[3] the South African writer Nadine Gordimer, who regarded La Guma as "the most talented black novelist since Peter Abrahams,"[4] believed it was not possible for a white writer like herself to write from within "particular areas of black experience" and because of that white readers

cannot create black characters. The same thing applies the other way about. But there is that vast area of our lives where we have so many areas of life where we know each other only too well, and there I see no reason why a black writer can't create a white character or a white a black.[5]

There is a fine point being attempted here although at first sight it might appear contradictory. In fact Gordimer doesn't quite bring it off, to my mind, and in response to a question later seems to retreat, saying there "is something beyond the imaginative leap." But what could that be? Is there something beyond imagination? This suggests a difference in essence, *a priori*, between 'white' and 'black'. Surely not.

It has to be remembered that Gordimer was replying in an interview directly and to the best of my knowledge did not have the benefit of being able to work out her comments on the page. If she had, to risk presumption, she might have brought in the considered use of basic structural techniques like the first and third-party narratives, and developed her argument from there. In a straightforward manner, third-party narrative allows the writer to create characters from the outside, where 'skins rub against each other.' This allows the writer to draw back from certain areas of experience, the sort which are to the fore psychologically and seem to demand the creation of character from the inside, more commonly wrought by the writer through first-party narrative, although other methods are always possible.

Alex La Guma wrote at least four novels; at the time of his death they were available in Heinemann's African Writers series, just about the most exciting list of English-language writing available anywhere, but difficult to get a hold of and in 1985 not a solitary work by him was available in Europe's largest reference library: Glasgow's Mitchell Library.

I managed to read two of his novels, on which basis I took Lewis Nkosi's point, that La Guma is only "a competent novelist who after the flashing promise of that first collection of stories seems to have settled for nothing more than honourable, if dull, proficiency."[6]

The Stone Country is an extended version of the short story *Tattoo Marks and Nails*. It is written in the third-person and is based on the writer's personal experience of prison. There are many good things about the novel but it has its defects, including a bit of a rushed, fairly predictable ending. But Yusef the Turk is a fine character and the Casbah Kid also, though occasionally La Guma glamourises a little too much. The converse of that is the deadened Butcherboy, a creation that only manages to get beyond the stereotype of 'hulking bully'.

The central character is George Adams, in prison for belonging to an illegal organisation which in the case of La Guma could simply have been the Communist Party since it had been banned for forty years by the fascist regime then in power. The novel is certainly 'competent' and La Guma's dialogue and working of the relationships between the prisoners often rises to the standard of the early stories. He uses the third-party narrative in a restricted fashion, rarely attempting to get within characters other than George

Adams: we are seeing how folk act rather than how they think – which lies at the root of Gordimer's point as far as I understand it, speaking as a writer and taking the positive angle. This form of narrative provides a structural base for the reader unfamiliar with prison life in South Africa and allows us to be with George Adams in his dealings with an environment alien to him.

La Guma's last published novel seems to have been Time of the Butcherbird which appeared in 1979; this ended a silent period of seven years. His other two novels are And a Threefold Cord and In the Fog of the Seasons' End. An anthology, Apartheid, and an account of his travels in the USSR, A Soviet Journey, do not seem to be available, though both are mentioned by his publisher.

According to the publisher's blurb for Time of the Butcherbird, the author gives "a rounded picture of all the people in a small community inexorably moving towards tragedy." I think this is what La Guma intended but I also think he fails and that he fails in a predictable way. He uses the third-party narrative voice but does not restrict it. Instead he sets out to give the psychological workings of assorted individuals; 'blacks', 'whites' and 'coloureds'. This was a very difficult undertaking. He fails, he falls into the trap of stereotyping. The poor white woman, Maisie Stopes, and the militant black woman, Mma-Tau, are clear examples of this: the former is a kind of sleazy 'semi-slut' while Mma-Tau is a vast 'Mother Earth'.

It has to be said that the writing is hurried, often clumsy, and obviously required a deal more work on the editing. The person for this would have been La Guma himself. Failing that people at the publisher's office might have performed the job as well as they could. (And did the writer censor himself in The Stone Country, or was it done by another hand?)

La Guma's very fine skill lay in his dealings with day-to-day existence, his precise and "concrete observation which is the correct starting point for all materialists."[7]

The high point in his novel Time of the Butcherbird is the introduction of Shilling Murile from the time that he is "sitting in the ditch" straight through until the end of the period he spends with the shepherd Madonele, some 4,000 words later. This is the stage when they move off together "through the crumbling dunes, smelling the smoke." This long section is beautiful. It is a brilliant piece of writing. It shows the true mark of the artist.

This is La Guma at his best and puts him in the higher rank. The skill he shows here indicates why he would have felt himself capable of trying a novel as ambitious as this. It was a risk, but he failed. In that marvellous short story A Matter of Taste the risk was an easy sentimentality but he avoided that and succeeded.

Until the Sharpeville massacre in 1960 the focus of the liberation struggle in South Africa had been on campaigns of non-violent resistance. At Sharpeville "seventy five members of the South African police force fired about 700 shots into the ['perfectly amiable'[8]] crowd, killing sixty nine Africans and wounding 180. Most of them were shot in the back." The Pan Africanist Congress of Azania as well as the ANC became outlawed thereafter, and "new strategic perspectives were imperative."[9] Oliver Tambo put it another way: "There can be no compromise with fascists."[10] In 1993, the year before the first free election, I was fortunate to be in South Africa at a conference in Johannesburg organized by the ANC. The white racists were still in power and there was tremendous hostility towards what was happening. Two weeks before our arrival Chris Hani had been murdered by somebody linked to the regime. Then on the morning of our arrival Oliver Tambo died – Comrade O. T., the only name I heard used of him, and with such affection.

The South African Communist Party had been banned since 1950 and it and the ANC now strengthened links. A year later its "leaders . . . formed a military organisation known as uMkhonto we Sizwe (MK) 'to carry on the struggle for freedom and democracy by new methods.'"[11]

> There are many people who feel it is useless and futile for us to continue talking peace and non violence against a government whose reply is only savage attacks against an unarmed and defenceless people.[12]

In response to this development of the liberation struggle the white racist regime stepped up its campaign of terror and oppression and "its utilisation of emergency military and police powers . . . marked the beginning of a new phase in South African politics."[13] Within three years security forces had captured and jailed seven leading figures. This took place at a farm in the suburb of Rivonia, not far from Johannesburg; the captured figures included Govan Mbeki, Nelson Mandela and Walter Sisulu.[14]

It was a massive blow to the liberation movement, one from which it did not recover for many years. Thousands of people were forced into exile, amongst them Alex La Guma. He had engaged actively in politics since the 1950s and, following five years' house arrest and bouts of imprisonment without trial, he left the country. From that period and until his death in Havana he worked on behalf of the ANC. In between times, where and when possible, he engaged as a writer of fiction and non-fiction.

The best artists always take risks. Realism is the term used to describe the 'detailing of day-to-day existence' and most writers who advocate social change are realists. One of the areas of exclusion under the South African Censorship Act is the 'advocation of social change'[15] and the writings of La Guma have always been banned there, in his home country.

Nothing is more crucial nor as potentially subversive as an appreciation of how the lives of ordinary people are lived from moment to moment. This is what we get in art.

Ordinary people. In the African Horn the children of ordinary people are eating insects to stay alive. It is a fact of existence so alien to other ordinary people that it cannot be admitted; there is an element lacking, a sort of structural base that does not allow us to be with folk for whom starvation is death and not simply a concept. To face such a fact in literary terms seems to be possible only in the work of a writer prepared to encounter the minutiae of day-to-day existence. And as far as I can see any formal advances in prose have occurred directly because of that struggle. Formal advances and 'imaginative leaps' may not be the same thing but they cannot easily be prised apart.

As long as art exists there are no areas of experience that have to remain inaccessible. In my own opinion those who think otherwise are labouring under a misapprehension which will lead to a belief that it is not possible to comprehend someone else's suffering, that we cannot know when someone else is in pain, that whenever I close my eyes the world disappears. It is an old problem. It has been kicking about in philosophy for several centuries. Just when it seems to have gone it reappears under a different guise and leads to the sorts of confusion we get in discussions to do with art and realism – naturalism – relativism – modernism – existentialism – and so on. One good example of this concerns the work of Franz Kafka.[16] He is one of the greatest realists in literary art of the twentieth century. His work is a continual struggle with the daily facts of existence for ordinary people. Kafka's stories concern the deprivation suffered by ordinary people, ordinary people whose daily existence is so horrific other ordinary people simply will not admit it as fact, as something real, as something verifiable if they want to go and look. The great artists manage to bend our line of vision so that we see round corners and perceive different realities; they work in the minutiae of day-to-day existence, trying to gain access and make manifest the darker areas of human experience, and suffering.

Most artists from oppressed or suppressed groups are under pressure of one kind or another. Time becomes the greatest luxury. Without time the work just cannot be done properly. To read Time of the Butcherbird is to see a writer of enormous potential labouring to perform a workaday chore. But to criticise the lack of development in Alex La Guma's prose[17] is to assume certain general points concerning the role of the artist in society.

La Guma would not be divorced from his culture, no matter how hard white racist authority tried to achieve it. His whole background was one of radical commitment. His father was James La Guma, a former president of the Coloured People's Congress. Both he and Alex were members of the Communist Party throughout their lives and in 1955 they were involved in the formation of the Congress Alliance. This comprised the Indian Congress, the African National Congress, the Coloured People's Congress and the white Congress of Democrats. When the treason trials took place in 1955–61 Alex was one of the 156 leaders of the Alliance to be charged by the State. Then began the series of imprisonments and house arrests which only ended with his departure from South Africa in 1966. He lived in London from then until 1979, although the literary people in control down there seem never to have noticed. For several years he was secretary of the Afro-Asian Writers Organisation (in 1969 he had won their Lotus Prize for literature).

Exactly one week after La Guma's death the poet Benjamin Moloise was murdered on the gallows by South Africa's white racist authority. Only a few years before that another good young poet, Arthur Nortje, committed suicide – in Oxford, England. He was awaiting deportation, enforced deportation; he was being sent 'home' against his wishes.[18]

In Roque Dalton's *Declaration of Principles*[19] the poet can only be – as far as the bourgeoisie is concerned – a clown, a servant or an enemy. In South African society there was no alternative role available, whether for ordinary people or ordinary poets.

Alex La Guma died of a heart attack in 1985. From February 1990 the ANC was 'unbanned' by the fascist South African State and could no longer be called a 'terrorist organization', not even by the Prime Minister of Great Britain, at least not publicly. On the 11th of the same month Nelson Mandela walked free. In October it was "announced that 20,000 exiles would be allowed to return" home. Meanwhile the ANC "demanded an end to 'the shocking inhumanity' of police action in rural areas."[20] A year on, in 1991, they were seeking "a multi-party commission of inquiry into the authorities' involvement in the violence and the secret funding of political activity, as well as the public dismantling of all special counter-insurgency forces."[21] Into October 1992 "the Goldstone Commission reports the finding of a secret operational centre run by Military Intelligence and seizes plans to destabilise the

ANC."[22] Then in January 1993 "the ANC . . . released a CIA memorandum approved for release under the US Freedom of Information Act, which stated that South Africa [had] detonated its first nuclear bomb with the assistance of Israeli scientists – off the Cape Atlantic coast in 1979."[23]

In April 1994 the ANC was voted into power in the first free election and have been the party of government ever since.

As a personal footnote; one of my treasures is a telegram I received from Alex La Guma himself in early 1983. In those years I was Writer in Residence to Renfrew District Libraries and organized the Paisley "Writers Weekends." I had sent him an invitation to come and give a reading of his work. Unaware of his whereabouts I sent it c/o the ANC office in London. Much later came the telegram reply from Havana, and I found the irony very cheery indeed:

THANK YOU FOR INVITATION FORWARDED ME FROM LONDON STOP REGRET THAT AS AM RESIDENT IN CUBA WILL FIND IT DIFFICULT TO JOIN YOU STOP HAVE A GOOD WEEKEND STOP ALEX LA GUMA

In the Spirit of Harry McShane

In 1991 I was invited to give a talk in Glasgow by the Socialist Workers Party (SWP), as part of the centenary celebration of Harry McShane's life. Aspects of the politics in this memoir are of that era. The event was chaired by Tommy Gorman not long before he resigned from the party. At that time he was Convenor of Shop Stewards at Leyland DAF. In earlier times this Clydeside factory was known as the Albion Works and Willie Gallacher had held the same Convenor's position. A couple of years on from the centenary meeting a huge strike took place at Leyland DAF, led by Gorman by virtue of his role. The management sought to sack him during the strike. Eventually they succeeded. Since then he has gone on to become one of the foremost figures in the struggle on behalf of the victims of asbestos abuse.

I never met Harry McShane personally and at the time knew little about his life.[1] Through my recent acquaintance with Hugh Savage and Leslie Forster I had begun to learn more. The one thing they insisted on was the old man's open mind.

This had isolated him within the Communist Party of Great Britain (CPGB), of which he had been a prominent and respected member since the 1920s. Hugh Savage gives an idea of this when he describes himself as 'a good wee Stalinist', until he met Harry McShane.[2] In the immediate post-war years, finally, keeping an open mind led to his resignation. Savage and Forster and a couple of others were side-by-side with him in that. That was back in 1951.

The resignations of the group caused a sensation in left-wing circles. Les Forster tells of "a meeting in Bill McCulloch's house, along with Hugh Savage, Matt McGinn, Harry McShane . . . we were paid a visit by the Trotskyist leader Gerry Healy . . . to recruit every one of us into his Movement. He even had in his pocket a press statement, announcing that we had thrown in our lot with The Workers Revolutionary Party." They met with bitter hostility. Such 'disloyalty' was unforgiveable within the CPGB. Forty years later there was very little change; they were still faced by that hostility, and the same question put to them: "Why did you leave the Party?" McShane's response was to reverse the question: "Why did you stay in it?"

But his resignation from the Communist Party had more personal repercussions. He no longer had a job as full-time organiser, a job he had held for years. Not only that, he lost the use of the wee room and kitchen living space attached to the CPGB branch in the Gorbals. This at the age of sixty-three. He had to go 'back on the tools'. He was an engineer to trade and managed to find work on Clydeside. And he returned to

Marx, especially Volume 1 of Capital, to re-examine matters on the basic 'first principles' level.

In the USA the philosopher Raya Dunayevskaya had developed her own thought, showing "Humanism to be the red thread connecting all four decades of Marx's development . . . Marxism was nothing if not a theory of liberation,"[3] liberation of the individual, freedom from wage-slavery. Dunayevskaya was Chairperson of News and Letters and a former secretary of Leon Trotsky. McShane was intrigued by her analysis and how the

preoccupation with what Leon Trotsky called "the small coin of concrete questions" has ever been the road away, not from the Mystical Absolutes of Hegel, but from the revolutionary principles of Marx. It was so during the life of the Second International. It characterized the Third International following the death of Lenin. The theoretic void in the Marxist movement has persisted to this day, when mindless activism thinks it is the answer to today's hunger for theory . . . It has always been my belief that in our age theory can develop fully only when grounded in what the masses themselves are doing and thinking.

This leaves economics as a means to an end where 'the end' is a society in which dignity and self-respect may be taken for granted. That was true liberation; human beings living freely, developing as whole individuals, making use of their imagination, their creativity, their power to conceptualize, to theorize. This awareness of the reality of manual labour and wage-slavery on the intellectual development of the individual is something he shared with John La Rose.[4] Both La Rose and Dunayevskaya were close friends of C. L. R. James.[5]

McShane corresponded with her: "I kept reading all I could get my hands on and finally came to the conclusion that you were correct." One thing he knew was the intellectual connection between Marx and the Scottish Enlightenment thinkers, in particular the four professors Adam Ferguson, William Robertson, John Millar and Adam Smith. This is the subject of a fine essay by Ronald L. Meek: *The Scottish Contribution to Marxist Sociology*, reprinted as a single essay pamphlet. I have it in my possession, passed on to me by Hugh Savage. In this essay Meek observed of Adam Smith that "the more narrowly economic views of The Wealth of Nations have usually been emphasised at the expense of the general sociological system of which they were essentially a part."[6]

McShane's long distance friendship with Raya Dunayevskaya[7] endured from 1959 until 1983. The bulk of their correspondence is deposited at The National Museum of Labour History in Manchester. It provides the core of The Harry McShane Collection 1959–1988.[8] Occasionally when she came to Britain she stayed at Hugh Savage's home in the east end of Glasgow.[9]

He and Leslie Forster were irritated by the relationship McShane had with the Socialist Workers Party in the latter years of his life. They were around thirty years junior to McShane and their friendship had endured since the 1940s. For the Harry McShane Centenary event each had been asked to contribute from the platform, and each had rejected the invitation. They referred to one occasion in particular when Harry McShane had been allotted ten minutes to speak at a public meeting, and Tony Cliff had fifty.[10] Although that seems not to have bothered McShane it certainly bothered Hugh Savage and Leslie Forster. In line with this I thought to reject my own invitation but they said not to do that, it was their preference that I spoke.

It was my policy to speak whenever asked by any left-wing party and to do so as openly as possible. I had my own opinion of the SWP as a body which was fairly negative from a left-wing stance but in mainstream circles I would not have criticised them. Besides that I was friendly with a couple of their members, including Tommy Gorman who had known Harry McShane towards the end of his life.

There was a decent crowd at the Centenary meeting. Hugh Savage and Leslie Forster were sitting in the front row. I designed my talk towards the idea of keeping an open mind, in the spirit of Harry McShane, not allowing yourself to be 'guided' by party dictat. I was in non-negative rather than optimistic mood in my approach, hoping a couple of party hacks might shift uneasily on their chairs.

Harry McShane was very close to John Maclean and occupies a crucial position in Glasgow's radical history. When he broke with Maclean it was to join the CPGB. I knew he was strong on theory and the exploration of ideas. As an engineer to trade he was what we call 'self-taught'. This kind of education happens in the workplace or the streetcorner; in your kitchen or somebody else's kitchen, maybe a café or the early stages in the pub – I stress the early stages. You learn through dialogue, by talking and listening, by debate; by working your way through ideas, arguing them out with friends and comrades. With a bit of luck somebody points you towards a book and you start following that through. The very last thing you need is a closed mind, you must be open, and receptive to fresh ideas; not only new ideas but old ones too.

Before you start to fight you've got to have some idea of why, why you are fighting. Otherwise it's meaningless. You've got to try and see things. You've got to recognise there's a problem. You've got to get to know why the problem exists. When you do that you are being critical, you are being analytical. You know not to take things at face-value, just because somebody in authority tells you it is true. We know the leader of the Labour Party in Glasgow is telling lies when he declares that he *represents* the Glasgow public and this entitles him to continue making decisions that can only end in a quite grievous future. Don't think I'm exaggerating about the grievous future. This is where such an abuse of power leads. The gang now in charge at Glasgow's Council Chambers have the sort of control that the average Member of Parliament down at Whitehall only dreams about. Local politicians don't have to cope with those permanent structures of State faced by MPs. The British State is never too upset when the left concentrates its attention on so-called national issues rather than local affairs. Local is particular and national is general, moving to the abstract, and the more abstract the better as far as the State is concerned.

When the leader of the local Labour Party or any of our so-called 'elected representatives' makes that kind of stupid statement we know intuitively they're telling lies. The difficult bit is sorting out where exactly they're doing it. After all, the way our society operates, its basic assumptions and so on, there is an element of truth in what they say. So how do you get to the bottom of it? One way is to examine what they are saying in light of what they do.

Sooner or later you have to sort out the basics, the starting point, you wind up having to work out what they mean by words like 'democracy', what they mean by 'representation'. All of that.

I have been involved with the group called Workers City for more than a year now, since early 1990. Many of you here this evening will have heard of the group and hold opinions about it, not all complimentary. That's fair enough. The central factor which I think binds those involved is the wish to expose political corruption here in Glasgow, particularly on the mainstream left, where most of the hypocrisy and double-dealing exists. What this entails is gathering information and trying to get it made public. That's what keeps me involved anyway.

I have to stress that Workers City is not a party, it is a small campaigning group (with its own internal problems), and sometimes it operates as a support group. We publish The Glasgow Keelie, a wee newspaper which amounts to the four sides of an A3 sheet. We try to publish this roughly once every four to six weeks and we've initiated some campaigns. The most widely known last year was the one supporting Elspeth King, curator of the People's Palace, the famous old museum on Glasgow Green. We aimed to draw attention to the fight she and her assistant were engaging in to safeguard the integrity of the museum; not for any purpose to do with their careers, but to safeguard the place itself, with its tremendous collection of socio-historical relics. They rightly regard this wonderful collection as the property of the people of Glasgow, to be held in trust for future generations.

This campaign failed inasmuch as Elspeth was demoted and has since left Glasgow, and they sacked her assistant.[11] A new curator and new assistants were brought in from outside Glasgow to perform the necessary work, whatever the Council asked of them, including the dispersal of much of the collection.

So that campaign must be counted as a defeat. The other Workers City campaign to receive media attention was the one to save Glasgow Green from the private developers. That campaign was won. But such victories are never final. People need to be vigilant. The Council authorities will try again sooner or later.

For myself it has been interesting to see the amount of hostility such a small group of activists can arouse by concentrating on local issues. Of course the hostility that interests me most is the kind that comes from the mainstream left.

I should say that if anybody wants to ask questions on any aspect of Workers City later on, during the Q&A, then they are welcome. There's a few other folk from the group here in the audience.[12]

Just now I do not want to talk about the Labour Party machinery and how it manifests itself in Glasgow City Chambers. People here know it is corrupt. In paying attention to certain issues you map that corruption and try and show what its effects on the community are or could be. There is an extension of this point: local politics are a turn-off for a great many people, but the paradox is that struggle usually begins on your own doorstep.

When you map corruption at a local level the network always spreads out the way. Paul Foot here has been involved in what is known as 'the Colin Wallace Affair' which features political corruption at the highest level.[13] His involvement had to start somewhere and I believe that it started from a letter landing on his office desk one day. From that point on, at the risk of being presumptuous, I would be surprised to hear him say he followed any specific course of action. I would doubt whether there was any 'specific course of action' to follow – apart from keeping an open mind and being as thorough as possible. In such a situation it seems to me that no other approach would work.

I am reminded of Noam Chomsky who about four years ago gave a series of lectures in Managua, Nicaragua. During one discussion he was asked by a member of the audience about dialectics, about the dialectical method and its importance to him. Chomsky said he had never quite understood what dialectics were. Then he said to the person asking the question: But if it works for you then use it.

One of these simple truths. Although the more you look at it the more complicated it gets. An aspect of what he means has to do with the idea that there is no unified theory which will explain everything. Such a thing is not even a possibility. Much of the revolutionary work Chomsky did in linguistics and the study of mind more than forty years ago concerns that very point. About the best we can hope for is being able to demonstrate that this theory over here works and that one over there doesn't. We might use a particular method to demonstrate the point, but other methods will come along. As far as the world is concerned, let alone the mysteries of the universe, there is no one system that will ever explain that. No one idea, no one person, none of that sort of stuff. Chomsky is attacked and marginalized by the right. He is also attacked and marginalized by folk on the left, and this is far more interesting. Of course he is an American middle-class academic and that is plenty for some people on the left. Chomsky's own education was far from orthodox and he might be better described as a self-taught academic.

The official education system does not provide people like Harry McShane with their education either. Not then and not now. That is not its purpose. Its purpose is the opposite; the official education system is designed not to educate. The 'self-taught' school exists in spite of the official one. The official one is a crucial part of the British State. We should not be surprised to discover that it fails to educate young people properly.

The education system is the first stage in a lifetime process of state propaganda and disinformation, the earliest battle in the psychological warfare the State wages against the people. It destroys our enthusiasm for learning. Instead of opening our minds it seeks to close them. When most working-class people leave school they never want to see another book in their life. Reading 'seriously' is a form of punishment. Education itself is seen as punishment. You have to fight to rediscover the excitement of learning. Any book you pick up is in spite of the system. Our kids have to steal what education they can. But what the State cannot stop is our access to books. It tries to in different ways but it is doomed to failure in that one respect at least.

What I am now stressing, in the spirit of Harry McShane and his friends and comrades, is not so much the importance of ideas, but the importance of the *exploration* of ideas. Because that is at the heart of radical politics. And people like McShane knew that and his peers also knew that, and I'm talking about John Maclean and others – the party line was never enough. This partly explains, further, why Maclean himself ended as he did, alone but for a handful of comrades, struggling against the ruthless retribution of the British State. Those men and women laid the utmost stress on that. You take nothing on trust without making inquiries, especially if it carries the label 'official'. And ultimately it does not matter if this idea is 'left-wing' or 'right-wing'. If it is 'official' you must be wary. You must see for yourself whether it is true or not. Enter into it with an open mind. If it works use it. If it doesn't then dump it. There is no authentic movement without that central critical element, that side of skepticism. I have not read a great deal of John Maclean's writings either but like most of the great radical thinkers and activists, in what I have read, he is – first and foremost – a *critical* mind. It is never enough to take what you are handed on a plate, you need to work it out for yourself.

The power of radical ideas is one of the strongest weapons we have on the left. And we do not have many. As soon as we stop exploring them we are as well burying them – and Highgate Cemetery[14] is as good a place as anywhere, because that is all it is, a cemetery.

The right-wing has very few ideas. And that is one sound reason for its continued success. Its only goal is to keep power. All its wealth and resources go toward that. It strikes me too that the current controversy about the so-called entry of the so-called far-right into the Tory Party underlines the point. Throughout its history we hear tales of far-right entryism. Usually they get away with it which speaks volumes in itself about where the establishment stands. But one feature of the far-right as far as I can see is how they attempt to explore ideas. These are not fresh ideas, they centre on the acquisition and use of power. But State pragmatists know this is dangerous. Ideas can weaken the power base. The Labour Party is Her Majesty's Most Loyal Opposition and therefore serves an important function. The far-right also has a function, as far as the British State is concerned, its function too is service. Those in servitude are allowed to think for themselves, but giving voice to these thoughts is a different matter; preferably not within hearing and, unless requested, never in public.

I used to think the British State would hang onto the monarchy at all costs, but I no longer think that. I can envisage them dumping that too, sooner or later, not quite in the way Margaret Thatcher got dumped but it's horses for courses, whatever is necessary. Thatcher was fine when she played the game; fine for that period in the mid 1970s through the mid 1980s when reaction needed an enforcer, when hoary old chestnuts like the 'Russian bogey' or 'loony left' needed fresh oxygen breathed into them. But once Thatcher started chasing ideas she too became dangerous. She described John Major as a man without ideas. But she was wrong to attack him for it. A person without ideas is exactly what State authorities require at that level. And to that extent a character such as Major is nearer the Reagan-like figure, a puppet. Those in control of the State insist on puppets where possible. Certainly Margaret got the message, just as the far-right will also get the message, in one way or another: until the next time.

I mentioned earlier the Campaign to Save Glasgow Green, the very place where generations of people have gathered to air and address their political grievances:

One hallmark of an oppressed society is the lack of public meeting places. In many countries in the world the state considers the church 'dangerous'. But in these countries you also find that the public have no other places available. It is not so much that religion is a threat: the threat comes from people gathering together. If talk is cheap dialogue is dangerous. It leads to action. This is why in times of domestic crisis the state do not allow groups of folk to hang about chatting at street corners; 'mobs' of four or more people are moved on by the police, otherwise they get done for 'loitering' – with intent to start a revolution. The authorities prefer a situation where the only meeting place is the pub. By the time you've talked your way through the problem you're too drunk to do anything about it.[15]

Glasgow Green is not only a prime site for the cash profit brigade, it is potentially dangerous, a threat to local security. Why? Because it is a place where people meet and talk, like the Citizens Rights Office and the Unemployed Workers Centre in Edinburgh or the tiny Clydeside Action on Asbestos office down the Briggait – never mind all the other community-based advice-centres that the Glasgow City Council are trying to close down. It is contemptible. Here we have a Labour-controlled authority, implementing Tory strategy, closing down places where working-class people go for help, places where working-class people meet. And when people meet they communicate, they explore ideas.

Ideas are not closed entry systems. You do not knock them down for the sake of it but you have to challenge them and be allowed to challenge them. If they can stand the light of day then fine. But we should not take them on trust. If you think you have a theoretical basis then find it doesn't bear scrutiny because of the actions being taken, actions speaking louder than words, you have to give up the idea, you cannot fight with a bag of wind and that is all these ideas amount to, party lines, political theories that override the lives of actual people. A bag of wind is the first target destroyed by the enemy, you don't need to fight it. It's full of air, a safety pin bursts it.

There is a stage where the leadership has the power. But if this is by consent then where comes the power except through the 'idea'. Yes, and the 'idea' is not to be challenged. That is an essential part of the 'idea'; so too leadership of the party. Have faith my child.

You see how the closed system operates. To get to the leadership you must get to the 'idea'. But the only way is through the leadership, because they hold the 'idea' which you are supposed to accept without question. And I am not just talking about the Glasgow Labour leader's control in the Council Chambers, nor the leader's control at national level. It is the party machinery that pushes people so morally and politically bankrupt into power. This system only works by placing the greatest store on minds that are not allowed to question, as events in Eastern Europe have shown all too clearly: sooner or later people get to the bottom of it, then reject it. At some point a quasi-socialist totalitarian state finds there is nothing to do except hand over the key to the cabinet. But of course the situation in Eastern Europe is not the same as here although if you live in Glasgow you have been getting an insight into how it might operate for quite a long while.

On the real left, the non-mainstream left, we have a situation where groups, parties and factions are divided by ideas and too often waste their time polishing them up, sticking them back in the display cabinet then locking the door. Here at this event, about myself for instance, people in the SWP will say, why have him come and talk? Outside the SWP people will say why is he talking on an SWP platform? And tomorrow on the platform at the anti-poll tax rally at George Square, outside the doors of the great halls of Glasgow City Council, something of mine is going to be read by an actor[16] and the same sort of comments and questions about myself will come from people involved with Militant, and the RCP, and the WRP, and the anarchist groups: and et cetera, it is a familiar pattern.

And since this night is a tribute to Harry McShane, who was pleased to speak on the SWP platform on many different occasions, it has to be faced that his friends are still angry about the way he was treated latterly. These things have to be confronted. If we do not confront them then there is no way forward. Such matters can only be settled in dialogue. We cannot afford to let dialogue become a lost art, not on the left, our networks and channels of communication must remain open.

It is not possible to construct truth out of one idea or one set of ideas, one individual or one set of individuals. Ideas do not belong to anybody. Every idea that ever has been was shaped collectively, by the dead as well as the living. If we take one we do not have to take them all; and we can take part of one and leave out the other bits. If there is one thing worth reading in the works of Lenin or Trotsky or especially Marx, then it is the index. You do not have to go away and study all the writers and thinkers that they studied. But you must recognise that that is what they did. They explored, and kept on exploring. Nothing is sacred. That is not how it works. Ideas come from people and nobody is perfect.

The courage Jeff had

Jeff Torrington published only two books in his lifetime, one a novel and one a linked collection of stories. There is an exuberance in his work which is at its core literary and derives from his love for literature. Jeff was at home in art, in music, in philosophy, and most of all at home in literature. It was his, and his of right. This was the most powerful assault on that essential elitism that stops many from experiencing the pleasure, the excitement and joy that might lie in wait if we dare to engage properly with literature. Jeff was somebody who dared, and his great novel was his expression of that. The confidence Jeff had reveals something of the best of us and people respond to that in his work.

He was a literary man whose preoccupations were formal, and he was never afraid to laugh. There was a wholeness and maturity about Jeff and his writing that I do not see as typical. He accepted responsibility and created in that fashion. He was of a kind to whom young people also respond. His novel Swing Hammer Swing! has had an influence on such as Duncan McLean, Alan Warner, James Ferguson, Irvine Welsh and others, not only in Scotland but in the USA. In 2007 a

Baltimore-based magazine judged the "Scottish masterpiece" to contain "One of the funniest sex-scenes ever written . . ."[1]

It was wonderful seeing people in different parts of the world responding so readily to his work.

It is forty years since we met. In January 1979 I began as Writer in Residence to Renfrew District. Jeff came to a writers group I started at Paisley Central Library. He had tried different writers groups over the years. I was wary of him at first. I was thirty-three. Jeff was ten years older. Not only did he know as much, he knew more; and while he was less prejudiced he was at least as opinionated. I was working on a variety of projects myself and soon we were talking literature in a way that I was not used to doing with writers other than Alasdair Gray and Tom Leonard. I formed another writers group in Linwood, and one in Spateston, by Johnstone; and Jeff came along to each when he could.

We saw common ground in the formal problems we faced. In an interview with Deborah Orr,[2] Jeff said

One reason why I took so long to write Swing Hammer Swing! is that I wrote four or five different versions. I didn't have a voice at all to begin with. Third person was a liberation, but it didn't feel right. I wrote a version in American usage as well. The Scots so readily became fans of American culture that it sometimes seems like ours is body-bagged ready for dumping. I went back to first person, because that's how I felt comfortable.

At that time I also was working back and forth between third and first-person narratives, in particular with my novel The Busconductor Hines. Eventually the narrative had to exist in third-party and I remember heated conversations between the two of us about that, and Jeff settling on a first-person narrative for similar reasons, so that in the quote above, when he talks about 'feeling comfortable' I think he was also referring to the freedom this first-party allowed Tam Clay to be the guy he became. There are some great stories we read where the central characters become our friends as readers, some good, some not so good, others exasperating. 'Thomas Clay' was not Jeff Torrington, not even a 'thinly-disguised' one, but I have been fortunate to know both as pals.

There were the writers we both loved for what they did as story-tellers and as writers too, especially Kafka, Chekhov, Dostoevsky and Camus, and there were writers each of us enjoyed separately from the other. I respected the fiction of Hermann Hesse and Vladimir Nabokov but I was never able to read either for pleasure, unlike Jeff who enjoyed them both. He also read Camus, Sartre, Balzac and Stendhal in French and I envied him being able to read these great writers in their own language.

He never hid in these writers workshop groups and was generous with his time, generous with his criticism. He prepared his comments on people's stories and poetry individually, working his way through on a line by line basis. In those groups there can be demanding individuals. Jeff would be amused rather than annoyed. But we had fun too, and some fine conversation.

He had published some early short stories in the old Argosy tradition. He called them 'scorpions', 'scorpion tales', because they had the requisite "sting-in-the-tail". He didn't enjoy puns, he loved them. I fucking hate them! But he loved them, and the more stupit the better. He also wrote poetry and revue. His novels then in progress were Swing Hammer Swing! and Go Down Laughing which he never managed to finish but contains enough for some brave publisher to take a look. He also worked on the linked collection The Devil's Carousel which eventually was published in 1996.

I remember during my second spell as Writer in Residence to Renfrew District he missed a couple of the Monday night meetings at Paisley Central Library, later confiding he had appointments at the Southern General Hospital. Then he was diagnosed with Parkinson's disease. He was still in his forties. What an extraordinary and massive blow. Then he fought back, strengthened by the support of his wife Margaret who was his greatest champion. The pair married young, both Gorbals born and bred.

After that diagnosis, he undertook yet another rewrite of Swing Hammer Swing!. What courage Jeff had, and perseverance, like all great artists. He further completed The Devil's Carousel and continued his work on Go Down Laughing, a title he had before the onset of Parkinson's, and he continued the struggle over such a long, long period.

That sense of fun did not desert him. He used a typewriter for most of those difficult years and finding the right keys was problematic. He went through a lot of Tippex. It flew about the room like white paint. He said, I'm the first writer that ever needed a pair of dungarees.

Swing Hammer Swing! was an immediate success, not only lifting the prize for the Whitbread first novel category but its overall Book of the Year Award, in the face of strong competition, including Poor Things, a very fine novel written by Alasdair Gray.

The launch of The Devil's Carousel was held in Brendan McLaughlin's Clutha Bar. Jeff was no longer able to perform readings in public but he and Margaret were there. It was a special night, with musicians present and readings from his work by writer friends, of whom he had many. Other writers held him in great esteem.

A couple of years before he died Jeff had become very ill and his wife Margaret started reading sections to him of his unfinished novel Go Down Laughing. It still made him smile, still made Margaret smile. Me too. During the last period of his life I visited him in hospital and read sections of the manuscript to him on a couple of occasions.

He was a respected man in his own locale. He was big and powerful and handsome too, the kind of guy Glasgow women call 'a fine big fella' but he was also a man for friends and community: and he was a part of his own community, and enjoyed it greatly. He had been an employee in the local Rootes car factory. It isn't that he disliked football at all but Saturday afternoons were not spent on the football terracing but in the Clippens Bar, Linwood where the weekly 'philosophy club' met.

He died on Sunday 11 May, 2008 at 6.30am, more than twenty years after that first diagnosis. He had had such a hard time of it the last few of them, supported through it all by his wife Margaret. Heroes the two of them.

June's Laugh[1]

Our Black language is a political fact suffering from political persecution and political malice. Let us understand this and meet the man, politically; let us meet the man talking the way we talk; let us not fail to seize this means to our survival, despite white English and its power. Let us condemn white English for what it is; a threat to mental health, integrity of person, and persistence as a people of our own choosing.

And as for our children; let us make sure that the whole world will welcome and applaud and promote the words they bring into our reality; in the struggle to reach each other, there can be no right or wrong words for our longing and our needs; there can only be the names we trust and we try.[2]

June Jordan was the third person to whom I dedicated my Busted Scotch selection of short stories which was published in USA 1997. Tillie Olsen and Mary Gray Hughes were the others. I was fortunate to know all three and think of them as friends.

I was introduced to her work by Mark Ainley, better known for his involvement at Honest Jon's music store down Portobello

Road. In the mid-1980s he assisted in the organisation of literary and cultural events in Battersea Town Hall. A play of mine, In the Night, was performed there. The production was dreadful and I prefer to forget about it. On another occasion a lecture by Noam Chomsky sold out at the same venue. I went down from Glasgow along with others to hear him and make contact.

I also did a reading at Battersea Town Hall; part of a programme that included Tom Leonard, Agnes Owens and Kathy Acker, as well as June Jordan herself. In those days a good team of folk were around in London, organizing music and literary events, mostly associated with Compendium Books of Camden Town, a wonderful place. Mike Hart worked at the fiction section. Mike introduced me to Kathy Acker one afternoon. She was scouring the shelves and tables of 'hardboiled' private-eye fiction, hard-bitten cops and street-wise dames. Kathy enjoyed all that stuff and used it in her own work, in her own inimitable manner. She came to Paisley to take part at the old Writers Weekends I was organising in the early to mid-1980s. Kathy Acker and Agnes Owens sharing the bill: what a team. I hoped to bring June Jordan north but she never made it.

Nights with June were proper aesthetic events, and always political. She was a great artist: poet, essayist, activist and one hundred percent committed human being. Her generosity to younger writers was a byword. In American literature she is a seminal figure. I mean by 'seminal' here, that if you have an interest in a certain literary area there are writers you are obliged to read. If you remain in ignorance of their work then your interest in that certain literary area is not so serious as you might think.

Among women young and old, her work remains a beacon. In person she was a ray of sunshine. Really, when she entered a room, that was my experience. She was one of these individuals that people smiled to see. It sounds slushy and sentimental but I'm not finding a better way to say it. This presence she had derived from her own history, her work as a writer, what she had seen and been through, her total engagement; personality and so on, these lines shade into one another.

She took them all on, the horrors, whoever needed it, and she fought, she just fought and struggled and fought and struggled and that was that. Meanwhile she wrote and recorded: poetry, essays, interviews, dramas, dialogues, and beside all of this she was a teacher and mentor; one who led, truly, by example.

Young black women especially held her in awe. She was theirs. Her struggles were their struggles. The courage and determination are there in those early essays that begin from the brutal racism of 1960s New York, following "the murder of fifteen-year-old Jimmy Powell . . . half the size of the big, Irish cop wearing no uniform and electing to shoot a kid who allegedly held a pen knife."[3]

How on earth do we deal with that.

Anyone in doubt as to the significance of the title of her first essay collection, Civil Wars, soon discovers answers via the reality of 1960s New York, if you happened to be black and living in Harlem.

We were heading for the funeral of the boy . . . Literally
scores and scores of helmeted white policemen patrolled
the streets in hubs of 25 or 30 each . . . The presence of so
many . . . began to make me nervous, frightened, and angry.
We went to the 38th parallel: 132nd St. and 7th Avenue. Past
this corner no one was allowed. Buses began to arrive, taxis,
civilian automobiles, fire engines with sadistic screeching –
all vehicles jammed with policemen. The territory was clearly
invaded. I could not believe it when still another bus would
brake to a stop at that intersection and disgorge still another
hundred combatants. Overhead, helicopters dawdled and
dived and contributed to the unreal scene of a full-scale war
with no one but enemies in view . . . the bewildering multi-
plication of cops, guns in hand, helmets on their heads,
snarling expressions on their faces . . .[4]

This particular essay is difficult to read. And when I reread
it now after thirty years, and more than ten years since June
died, yes, I still find it difficult. Mark Ainley had sent me a copy
of June's essays on language, collected in her Moving Towards
Home: Political Essays (Virago Press, 1989). He also sent June
some of my work. It was the mid-1980s when I met her. Years
later she came to do readings in England and for two of those
she gave my name to the organisers as her support writer. The
first of the two readings took place at Brixton Town Hall. When
I arrived the queue reached round the building. What excitement! There were just too many people, the doors had to close

on them. It was the first and only literary event where I ever saw the organisers forced to ask a poet to give two performances so another audience could get the chance to hear her.

A younger Scottish writer was there, the poet Jackie Kay; eyes glowing, what excitement, Oh Jim! she said, and just shook her head. That summed it up. That was everybody. That was how they felt about June Jordan.

Ninety percent of that audience were young women. People were sitting on the floor and standing against the wall. It was a thrilling experience. This is how readings should be. It must have been weird when I appeared, this white guy with the Glasgow voice, first on. Why was I there? Why was I invited? Not all the looks were friendly. But for most people it must have been clear I was there with June, that I was reading with June, and would not have been reading with June unless she had given it the okay. People were polite and there were encouraging smiles from many. My novel How Late It Was, How Late had been published recently, amid much hostility, and I read from it. I cannot remember the section. How was it received? With patience, and with politeness, a rare smile, bemusement mainly. I was glad to reach the end.

When at last she walked out the audience response was close to overwhelming. She only had to stand there and smile, and that beautiful laugh she had. Who else ever could do that! Aesthetic integrity, political activism, commitment and solidarity, the will to change: those struggles and wars she had been through, and survived, and come out creating, doing her work and passing on to younger generations the need to continue doing just that, creating art, experiencing art; struggling and standing up for how it should be.

It took a while for the clamour to die down. The audience could not stop applauding and cheering. And that was before she began. Her response was laughter, she just laughed. The roof was going off. What a hero! She must have been a wonderful teacher. You get it from her essays. When she finished the performance the audience changed over, and she did it again. I wasn't there for that one.

The second occasion I read with her was in a theatre in the town of Oxford. There was a large audience and again I was reading from How Late It Was, How Late.

June was aware of the controversy surrounding the novel but had not reckoned on the extent of the hostility. Even during my reading, there were heckles. Oxford town too, this is what I was thinking, such incivility, one does not expect that in Oxford town, its academic integrity and so forth. And me a visitor too, from another country – more like another planet.

I kept on with it, and I heard this laughter. June was in the wings listening, she was just laughing.

The one thing I regretted after that performance is that I managed to control myself. Why the fucking hell did I not just dissolve into a fit of the giggles! Me! I should have laughed too. That is what she did, that is what she was doing. I should have joined in!

Ach well.

After her own performance I returned to participate in the Q&A session. That was at June's request. The organisers had assumed she would have been answering questions alone on stage and had laid out the one chair. When June told them they brought out a spare chair. I think she was still surprised by the venom directed against me from the audience, BBC Radio Three voices calling their questions:

Is there a place in fiction for those who know how to use grammar and spell the Queen's English correctly?

Now that you are accepted by the establishment do you still consider yourself a rebel?

The media give you all this free publicity to help you sell books: do you not think it churlish to whinge?

Is there a place in fiction for the Politically-Incorrect?

When the US edition of How Late It Was, How Late appeared I was over there doing publicity readings, around 1997. Three took place in the Bay area, including one at a bookshop in Berkeley where June then was living. I knew she was ill and made no attempt to contact her before my arrival. At the event there was not a bad audience. I was on my own for the reading. Afterwards there was a discussion in which I mentioned Franz Kafka. One young fellow asked me exactly what writings by Kafka was I talking about?

I treated this as an elitist attack, and one I was not unused to receiving. Generally I can spot them, those whose lower lips quiver in anger as they call: 'Mister Kelman, can you name any books you have read?'

It transpired I was wrong about the young fellow. He was fond of my work and had expressed the question badly. Unfortunately I didn't know that at the time, nor did most people in the bookshop who seemed of the same opinion as me. I took the question in the spirit I thought it was intended, which was absolute hostility, a rearguard battle on behalf of Standard English literary form, and I paused a while before responding.

The audience waited.

What was I going to do, jump off the platform and attack the fellow physically! How many strides would it take to get him by the throat! That was the bet if you were a bookie in the audience, smoke coming out my ears and so on.

Then from the back of the room came a gale of laughter, and I recognized this laughter immediately. June was here. I had not seen her in the audience and had no idea she would have been here, but here she was, sitting right at the back of the room. Who could mistake her laugh. I knew she was ill, but here she had managed along. I just laughed and gave her a wave.[5]

"Liberation begins in the Imagination"[1]

In 1987 a friend urged me to drop in at New Beacon Books next time in London and say hello to John La Rose. There were two or three 'next times' before I got round to it. It is awkward going to meet somebody you have not met before who is not expecting you and who most likely has not been advised of your existence; crossing social and racial borders does not help matters.

It happened one Saturday afternoon I had about five hours free time before travelling back to Scotland. I arrived at New Beacon about one o'clock. In the shop area was one other person, a younger man. He had a fair pile of books next to him on a table. He seemed to know his way around and I reckoned he was an employee. I had a small list prepared but could not find what I was looking for. He showed me where, then indicated other work he thought could be of interest. Afterwards I noticed him at the cash till paying for his books. He was not an employee at all, he was a customer.

I continued browsing. My own pile was steadily building; magazines, books and pamphlets. I called a halt and went to sort out the cash. It came to more than expected but included a couple of duplicates I was buying for a friend back in Glasgow.[2] The woman behind the counter had an accent I find difficult: middle-class English Home Counties, or so it sounded to me. At the same time I did not want to leave without trying: I asked if John La Rose was around.

She was quite matter-of-fact. John was semi-retired nowadays and was not keeping too well. I thought that a polite way of putting me off. It was not. She said I should call on him and gave me the home address. Outside the shop I reconsidered. Why was I dropping in? To say hello. Apart from that what had I to say? I could not think of anything. But here I was and why else had I come?

John answered the door. I cannot remember what I said although it wasn't as brief as 'hello'. He brought me in along the lobby past piles of books, piles of books and piles of books, and upstairs books were stacked on the sides of steps. In the wee kitchen he introduced me to somebody already sitting there: lo and behold the guy from the shop, the one I had taken for an employee; he was from East Africa.

The conversation I had interrupted continued. But not as if I was not there, and neither was I excluded. John glanced at me occasionally. It was up to me, if I had anything to say then say it. The conversation touched on various matters connected to Africa and the diaspora: economics, literature, liberation politics; issues

around language, the prominence of Hausa. It was really interesting; quite explicit politically, considering I was a stranger.

After about an hour and a half I could see John was tired. He
had been doing most of the talking and it was a strain. He
suggested myself and the other guy share the journey back to
where we were going, he to Brixton and me to Victoria for the
bus home to Glasgow. Whether he found the suggestion as
novel as myself I do not know; but off we went and made the
best of it. By the time we reached Victoria we were exchanging
addresses. (A year later when he and his partner were visiting
Glasgow they stayed overnight with me and Marie.)

In the space of that one short visit to New Beacon Books I
became friends with three people: one from East Africa, one
from Trinidad and one from middle-class England; it transpired that the woman in the shop with the middle-class English
accent was John's partner, Sarah White.

There was no internet in those days. Most of what I learned
of John's background I picked up directly or from his friends and
comrades, not through research. It was what was happening
there and then that was important. The New Beacon community had a mixture of art, culture and politics: an ethos. I was
drawn to this ethos so strongly it seemed like 'the missing link'.

Here I widen the context to include the Monitoring Group in
Southall. The principles, ideas and commitment of the people
involved around New Beacon and the Monitoring Group made
absolute sense to me, way beyond what is conventionally thought
possible in liberal-left Britain. This expressed itself in the

immediate impact it had on people's lives. Not consolation; and no, not "a change is gonna come." Nothing is goni come unless we make it happen. It was that sense of solidarity; a proper solidarity. People cared enough to assist in the struggle for justice. Hope was not passive. It developed through engagement, in the spirit of struggle. People asserted that fundamental right to existence, in defence of that and in absolute opposition to racism, and to make known publicly its effects and to confront mainstream Britain with its findings. Racists were murdering people and no one was being held accountable. Families walked in fear on a daily basis; unable to relax until their children returned safe and sound. Where have they been? Out playing with their pals; away to school, college, the leisure centre. Are they home yet? Did they say they were going to be late? Oh God, oh God.

It was extraordinary that this was happening in contemporary Britain.

Why were the criminals who perpetrated these horrors not brought to justice? Why was so little interest being shown by the British establishment? Why was the burden of proof being laid on the families, friends and communities of those whose lives were destroyed through the worst forms of racial violence? In very many such cases the work of the police and the Crown Prosecution Service appears designed to safeguard the perpetrators of these horrific crimes.

People had no choice but to strengthen their own communities[3] and find the means and commitment to sustain these communities in the face of attack. It is when we consider the violence unleashed against human beings for no other reason than difference – skin colour, ethnicity, racial origin – that the picture clarifies. These communities were, and to this day remain, communities of resistance; whether in Southall, inside London, Bradford, parts of Liverpool, of Manchester, Birmingham; wherever. Historical accounts of these areas of conflict are available online.[4]

The mutual friend who suggested I say hello to John La Rose at the start of this was Tarlochan Gata-Aura who also introduced me to his long-time friend from the Monitoring Group, Suresh Grover. Tarlochan was known in Edinburgh for his campaigning on behalf of the victims of racist attacks and for his work at the Citizens Rights Office. His approach to these areas brought a refreshing sense of priority, grounded on the rights of all human beings and his willingness not just to confront authority but to lay on it the burden of proof. In Scotland we are not used to asking the police, the immigration officers and other State authorities to explain or justify their actions. In common with most people in the United Kingdom we are taught to do as we are told and leave it to *'em as knows*, by one government or another. At the Citizens Rights Office in Edinburgh Tarlochan worked tirelessly and efficiently: so much so that the Labour-controlled regional council closed down the office. They did it in a typical act of cowardice, disguised as whatever it was, I cannot remember.

Later Tarlochan became Elaine Henry's right-hand man at Wordpower, Edinburgh's radical independent bookshop.[5]

In this wider context I knew where I was politically, culturally and strategically, assisted greatly by the work of the communities around New Beacon and Southall's Monitoring Group. It helped explain my frustration and general irritation with traditional left-wing circles in the UK, including many within the anti-parliamentarian left who appear to assume the validity of 'unity of the nation' arguments. Their vision, like the labour movement in general, seemed blinkered and naïve, unable to learn from other cultures, from other movements. The establishment talks of 'our' way forward and the vast majority of the white working-class believe themselves included in the term 'our', standing shoulder to shoulder with Sir Jim Ratcliffe, Lady Charlotte Wellesley, Sir Richard Branson, the Mountbatten-Windsors and all these knighted rockstars and celebrity entertainers. It is ludicrous.

I see now that I was piecing together a perspective derived from a finer or more thorough, more considered, experience of imperialism, and a push for justice that was not only 'in defence' but it was forward, onward, grab those fetters and chains and throw them to fuck, just rip them apart.

Some of this I knew personally from my background as a writer, as a member of my family and wider community. I knew what I was doing in language might be paralleled roughly with the work of other writers from diverse English-language literatures. It was the right to difference in individuals and communities, to reject assimilation and if enforced to resist it. That too lies at the heart of English-language literatures,

literatures that incorporate the rhythms and richness of indigenous linguistic forms. It is quite straightforward when seen in the anti-imperialist context.

I discovered that areas of John La Rose's background had touched me earlier than I thought; as far back as 1969 when I was working at the new Barbican development in London. I was a hammerman, one step up from a general labourer and it was the highest hourly rate I had ever earned. We worked a forty-six hour, five day week; the basic forty plus six hours overtime. Those forty-six hours were all that could be worked. The wage at the end of the week did not make you a millionaire but there were no complaints. The conditions were exceptionally good, including a subsidised canteen; potatoes, meat and gravy, the works. Was the grub tasty? Who knows. The quality was the quantity. Plus music while you ate from the guys at the next table: Derrick Morgan, Jimmy Cliff and Prince Buster, and the Ethiopians, the Skatalites, the Maytals.

The weird thing for me was the union, it was the old T & G, the Transport and General Workers' Union (TGWU).[6] I knew it of old as weak and toothless from my four times as a bus conductor. Not so here. Every Friday the lunch-break was cut to the half-hour, lunch followed by the branch meeting which was treated as compulsory. The workforce was Irish and West Indian, with a tiny sprinkling of Scots. The shop steward was a white Londoner, a very business-like guy. On the door into the canteen branch officials sold the Morning Star and whether or not your politics were to the left, right or centre of the CPGB it was good having the choice of a non-establishment line. This was the time of the long strike down at Thamesmead and construction workers travelled there in solidarity.

Soon after this I was married and my wife stopped working; we were expecting a child. On one wage we couldn't find a place to stay in London, nothing that made sense, not with alternatives. I quit the building trade and we returned to Glasgow. Back on the buses again; this time a driver, there was no other work. Once again I was a member of the TGWU. Once again the weekly wage I earned was only a liveable wage by cramming into one week's work the equivalent of two. We bade the boss good morning in the hope he would let us work seven days a week.

At the same time I no longer scorned the T & G itself. Working on the Barbican development taught me a lesson about trades unionism: any union can be strong; it is a function of individual branches. At the Barbican development the old TGWU was as strong as any; this because of its strength on the shopfloor. It was a hundred percent. Years later, through a chance remark from John, I discovered he had been a shop steward at the Barbican, on the very next site to my own. He was with Laings and I was with Turriff. And I happened to know that the outfit he worked with had the best conditions on the entire Barbican.

It was no coincidence. Nobody can convince me otherwise. They wouldnay have known what hit them! Here is a brief summary of what the shop steward John La Rose brought to the Barbican:

In the 1940s in Trinidad, he helped to found the Workers Freedom Movement and edited its journal, Freedom. He was an executive member of the Federated Workers Trade Union, later merged into the National Union of Government and Federated Workers. He became the general secretary of the West Indian Independence Party and contested a seat in the 1956 Trinidad general election after being banned from other West Indian islands by the British colonial authorities. He was also involved in the internal struggle of the Oilfield Workers Trade Union, siding with the "rebel" faction that wanted a more radical and democratic union. The rebels prevailed in the 1962 union election and John became their European representative, a position he held until his death.[7]

These were discoveries I was making of John long after I had come to know and respect him as a man, as a friend, as a comrade.

In the late 1960s in whatever free time I had, back home in Glasgow, I was working on my short stories. It would have been great to know John then and the wider New Beacon community. It would have helped prepare me for what lay ahead. Unless involved in Standard English literary form it is not enough to try for the highest literary level, you should prepare for life on the margins, for hostility, even ridicule.

And, of course, the economic reality which is penury unless working full-time elsewhere to pay for your 'self-indulgence'. The struggle is to support your family and accept that your family must support you.

And, if the art is literary, the practicalities: publishing, printing, distribution. Every writer should face up to startled, bored or hostile bookshop workers at some time in their life. Go and place copies of your work on a 'sale or return' basis, the deal where your books are tucked out of sight on the remotest of shelves, lying dormant for years. Here is where a peculiar phenomenon arises: the reluctance of writers to return to the bookshop, not only in case they didn't sell any, in case they did! A writer plucks up the courage to return to the bookshop and surreptitiously searches the shelves. Jesus Christ the books are gone! Have they been sold? Who knows. Nobody in the shop has ever heard of the damn thing, title or author. What is this, some newfangled ruse for shoplifting!

Those banal aspects of being a writer are compounded by 'difference' and part of what it means to be a different kind of writer, from a different kind of community, from a different tradition. Additional burdens, crucial burdens. The New Beacon ethos accepted "the artist as a totally vulnerable person engaged with other artists in a very vulnerable way."[8] This was part of how John related to writers; he recognized their vulnerability and tried to lift some of the burdens from them.

In 1966 John La Rose stopped work at the new Barbican site. He and Sarah whizzed around London on a motor scooter, transporting books, pamphlets and magazines. In this way they laid the foundations of New Beacon Books.

But there was so much more to it than opening a bookshop, no matter how radical, no matter how independent. "Besides being a publisher and writer [John and Sarah were] creating a whole autonomous community in the sense that you have the publisher, you have the writers [then] a sympathetic printer [plus] the shop to sell the work." Not only were they writing the books, the communities themselves, they were the customers, they were buying them. "So there's a complete self-sufficiency within this. It is, in a sense, the ideal." I said all that to John [9] and he was clear in his response:

> It happened by chance . . . partly because of the fact that here in London all the books I wanted to get and read, there was no place I could buy them. So I decided at some stage that we would really do the international book service. That was the very first book service of its kind ever done from the Caribbean. I was a Caribbean specialist so it meant that I did a booklist in French, Spanish and English. The very first catalogues we sent internationally to everywhere, so it meant that people came here all the time. This was still in the 1960s, people came to our house and worked downstairs, here in Albert Road, Finsbury Park . . .[10]

The Caribbean Artists Movement (CAM) was formed in that same year, 1966, and John was one of its three founder members, the other two being E. K. Brathwaite and Andrew Salkey. Its impact was swift and far-reaching. "The concept behind its informal structure was that of a community."

The sure basis for critical recognition by the establishment is assimilation. The call is unity at all costs. Difference is frowned upon. Show the authorities that you fit in. The greater the distance you place between your art and your home culture the more welcome you are at the gates of the establishment. And who knows, the guardians of that might pat yer head and grant entry. It is up to them, the merit of your art is irrelevant. Assimilation does not guarantee reward but sets you on the trail. One day they may reward you with a badge of empire. If you reject assimilation you will be punished by critical neglect, marginalization and the ever-diminishing means to survive as an artist.

The founder members of CAM recognised one fundamental issue, a most crucial and neglected effect of a marginalized culture, that for the artists there is no proper assessment of their creative output. Authentic criticism does not exist within a context defined by the dominant culture. Even where such creative output is noticed by the dominant culture it remains subject to it, judged by its criteria of what is 'good'.

During the 1950s and 1960s West Indian art was not unknown in mainstream circles, particularly its literature through the work of writers such as V. S. Naipaul, George Lamming and Derek Walcott, by Sam Selvon and Wilson Harris. Other artists were around but a critical context was missing. One of CAM's founder members was the poet and educator E. K. Brathwaite whose published work had received almost no attention whatsoever, neither from the dominant culture of the ruling British elite, nor from his own West Indian community: "Our problem is that we have been trained for over 300 years to despise [our] indigenous forms."[11] He might well have been discussing working-class Scotland, except we're into 400 years – since March 1603 or thereabouts.

Brathwaite had worked in Ghana during the period of Nkrumah and independence and become "immersed in the rural community life and traditional culture" of West Africa. At the first public meeting of CAM he argued the case for 'a jazz novel', that there was "a correspondence between jazz and contemporary Caribbean culture . . . the basic elements of word, image and rhythm; the nature of improvisation, of repetition and refrain;" and that the "oral tradition provided a model for West Indian literature . . . suggestive of an indigenous aesthetic for West Indian creativity and criticism."

These points on orature made by Brathwaite are striking and of major importance. I find it quite astonishing that they are so little known. The influence of Caribbean music was crucial. A·later public meeting was devoted to "Sparrow and the Language of the Calypso." John La Rose had already written on *kaiso*, calypso music.[12]

From an early age La Rose had been politically active in Trinidad. Former General Secretary of the Workers' Freedom Movement, he later held the same office for the West Indian Independence Party, "producing *Noise of Youth*, a fortnightly radio programme."[13] He was still in his twenties when he was forced into exile.

The third founder of CAM was Andrew Salkey who often met John at the same protests and demonstrations in London. Salkey was a freelance broadcaster (interviewing Martin Luther King on three occasions) and had a very wide network of contacts. As a student at London University he "devised an alternative learning plan for himself: 'I damn well wanted to talk to Jamaicans about Jamaica in the long poem I was hoping to write.'"

Of the broader political agenda Salkey made a key comment in relation to the different formations that existed during the 1960s – including the Black Power groups – that "no one group had it all, and I figured I had [to] serve nearly all and be useful to all."

CAM began as a means by which "writers, artists and people interested in literature, art and culture" could come together. Literature was the predominant artform but painters, musicians, sculptors and theatre workers were also involved. From informal gatherings held in the homes of members it was broadened out to public meetings and "included talks and symposia, readings and performances, art exhibitions and films . . . and a newsletter, bookselling and contact network."

It would be a mistake to place too great an emphasis on the founders. They were acquainted with a circle of committed individuals, artists and activists. One of its impressive aspects was the number and multiplicity of its participants, ranging from the elderly C. L. R. James to the young Ngugi wa Thiong'o and even younger Linton Kwesi Johnson. It was an extremely ambitious project and given the nature of its structure could not have succeeded without that wider commitment.

At CAM's first conference the historian Elsa Goveia argued in her keynote speech that artists have a choice

> between the inferiority/superiority ranking according to race and wealth and the equality which is implied by one man one vote [and] until then we cannot be really creative as individuals because our energies are going to be absorbed by the terrible job of working from two completely different sets of premises . . .

She also established the point "that the creative arts were at the forefront of . . . social change." This raised other questions, e.g. the "sort of art the committed artist should produce", "which art forms were most effective", "how the artist communicates and to whom", etc. The painters Aubrey Williams and Clifton Campbell who "both worked in predominantly abstract styles were concerned to defend it as no less socially committed than figurative painting . . ." Williams "asked for freedom for the artist to explore his own style: 'If our painters must grope and search and forge ahead, we do not as yet know the language they should speak.'" He spoke of his doubts on "narrative painting" as "hand-me-down missionary art" in danger of becoming "tourist representational art." The response from the audience to the work of the visual artists under discussion forced him to "conclude that the level of visual art appreciation among intellectuals is very, very low . . ."

The conference was such an exciting and unique event that how to follow it was a major problem. John La Rose was moved to write to Brathwaite that

> CAM is a movement . . . not a structure. We . . . have struck a chord. With such things, in my experience, people take out of it what they are looking for and bring what they must give. Then the communion is over. And it lives; and we inherit it; and it passes on. The vital spark of life and spontaneity, as I have discovered, in my own life, is not long-lasting. Glowing embers remain and we mistake it for fire. I mention this only that we would know what to expect.

That was in 1967, some five years before CAM's eventual demise. It is impossible to do justice to the impact and legacy of the Caribbean Artists Movement, both culturally and in the broader political context. Being within such a community in those years would have been dynamite for myself. The CAM aesthetic would have helped prepare those of us attempting to work from within the living voice and living tradition of our own communities. As a young writer it was my experience in that present period, as I was living it and working at it. Already I was running into problems in terms of language as a living thing, as a means of communication between human beings. In the very year CAM ended – 1972 – a printer in England refused to publish my first short story on the grounds of blasphemy, elsewhere described as "the language of the gutter."[14] A year later a small press in the USA published my first collection of stories. Nobody in Britain would have touched it, not that I knew about.

My 'payment' came by parcel post: two hundred copies of the book in lieu of cash. Next day I was driving a bus out the garage at 4 o'clock in the morning; just the thing to destroy any romantic illusions about being a writer. Empathy makes the difference, noting a shared experience, technical similarities. I saw it immediately and was drawn to the work of 'other colonials.' The struggle against the imposition of Standard English literary form was a class issue but there was another context, a wider context, that of imperialism, and the fight for indigenous survival.

In my local library in Theobalds Road, Holborn, 1967–69, did they stock a few writers from the Indian subcontinent and Africa? I seem to remember this was where I discovered the work of Mulk Raj Anand, among others.

Since my late teens, early twenties, outside of the European traditions I had been reading American writers who adapted standard form for their own use. In this respect I cannot say that any individual writer influenced me in particular. But it was very important to know that I was on the same track as these overseas writers. Here I can speak on behalf of others. In Scotland there is a tradition. A few writers were around who appreciated what was happening in alternative, English-language literatures. In 1975–77 Sam Selvon was Writer in Residence at Dundee University and made a huge impression, so much so that "[s]ince his death [in 1994], the Samuel Selvon Memorial Prize has been awarded each year to the most outstanding final year undergraduate English student at Dundee."[15]

In 1979 I landed a job as Writer in Residence myself, based in Paisley Central Library. There I came upon the work of Ayi Kwei Armah, Chinua Achebe, Sam Selvon, Amos Tutuola, Alex La Guma, Okot p'Bitek and others. Although using the English language, these writers were not out to assimilate, to emulate nor 'to be as good as.' They were attacking and the attack was formal, laying claim to language and the right to use it as necessary, where, when and how.

What they were doing was not new to me formally, not at all, but it strengthened my conviction and clarified the position. If I had known of the Caribbean Artists Movement ten years earlier then its impact would have been the greater, not in the practice itself but in making sense of the reaction.

There in Paisley Central Library I also found a couple of interesting catalogues which seemed responsible for most of the books in this 'Ethnic' section. One was the Heinemann catalogue for the African Writers Series and the other belonged to an independent publisher and distributor. I kept both in my room at the library. And when I left the Writer in Residence job I took both catalogues home with me. It was only in the last couple of years that I discovered I still have them. The small independent one turned out to be the 1979 catalogue, printed and published by New Beacon.

Any marginalized culture is a culture under attack. Accept the marginalization and act on it. Spread the information; share the experience; disseminate the knowledge. If the struggle succeeds it will succeed from the bottom up. Be methodical. Take what exists and lay claim to it, transcend it, get beyond it. You write, publish, co-publish or otherwise acquire the books, pamphlets, magazines, tapes or whatever; then you advertise, distribute and sell them, if possible in your own bookshop, a place where people will eventually drop in, just to say hello. No lines of demarcation, no restricted zones; outsiders may enter and are welcome. But the operation will function either way, whether new people visit or not. A certain commitment from within the community is required: with maximum commitment who knows where it may lead. As John said at the founding of the Caribbean Artists Movement: "liberation begins in the imagination." He died in 2006 but New Beacon Books remains in existence, and the George Padmore Institute thrives.[16]

Tillie Olsen was there

In 1997 I took part in a panel of Scottish writers at an Anarchist bookfair event in San Francisco organised by, among
others, AK Press. There is a strong literary tradition in San
Francisco, a radical tradition. Before the discussion started,
while the writers and audience were settling into their seats, I
noticed an elderly woman signalling my attention. She
approached the table and I went to meet her. I assumed she was
a distant relation descended from my great-aunt Margaret
(Mackenzie) Macarthur who emigrated from the island of
Lewis to Seattle in the 1920s. The extended family were living
throughout the west coast, mainly California, so when I went to
meet her I was preparing for a great cuddle. I had to confess
to her that I did not know her name but I knew she was a relation. She was not a relation at all, this elderly woman, she was
Tillie Olsen.

Tillie Olsen. Her work had been central for myself during
the previous twenty years, way back from the 1970s when
Mary Gray Hughes first recommended her work to me. Not
only did Mary Gray recommend her work she sent me her
own copy of Tell Me a Riddle. It had had an immediate

impact on myself, and I mean formally. Emotionally, yes; the expression of emotion is so concentrated in Olsen's work, an extraordinary tension. Tillie Olsen is one of those artists whose dramatic impact is so powerful that we have to pause in the reading, to recover. Chekhov is like that; the later Tolstoy. But as a young writer, then still in my twenties, it was the formal aspect I found so exciting. In future her work was in the first group of writers whose names I passed to Creative Writing students. Forget how to write, how do you fight: do you want to fight? Learn how to use a colon. Do you understand grammar? No, well this is your ammunition; you must have it at your disposal.

People wonder why someone who publishes one collection of four short stories has such an influence on generations of writers. *I Stand Here Ironing* is the first of the four. That story is just about unbearable for me now, forty-five years later as a grandfather with two daughters, and two grandchildren. But each of the four is a marvel. The title story is a masterpiece. I don't think it is a young person's story, not this young person anyway. I always appreciated it but it took a number of years for me to connect fully. I see it now, this immigrant's tale. An elderly couple coming to terms with the reality of old age, fighting to survive, fighting one another.

Olsen remains a hero for so very many women. Get to know her life and you will understand why. She wrote one novel, begun in her teens and finished in her forties. The kind of writer one continually pushes on other people, to the extent we have to renew our libraries all the time; we keep giving her books on loan and never get them back.

With Tillie there now with me I found nothing to say, nothing. The panel discussion was about to begin. I could not say anything to her. She gripped my wrist then returned to her seat. I had to leave the room. I went to the bathroom, washed my face, looked into the mirror. So, there ye are. I returned to the main space. Other writers were there on the platform: Alan Warner, Kevin Williamson, Irvine Welsh, musician and writer Brendan McLaughlin, also John Mulligan whom I had got to know lately. San Francisco had been his home for a long number of years. John had been introduced to Tillie personally by Maxine Hong Kingston, a very fine writer who also organised a Creative Writing workshop for US army vets, and was particularly supportive to those suffering the effects of post-traumatic stress disorder.

A few years earlier Silences had been published in England by Virago Press which is when I was first in contact with her. Tillie was around seventy years of age, but was making the trip to London to help launch the book, in company with her close friend, Adrienne Rich. One of the broadsheet newspapers sent a journalist to interview her, a woman. Judging by the finished piece the person had never heard of Tillie Olsen and detested most everything about her: integrity, honesty, moral commit-ment, left politics, frankness of expression. Perhaps it was her unwillingness to enter into a self-deprecating irony that most upset the journalist whose finished feature ridiculed the great

American writer in a most extraordinary show of upper middle-class English elitist prejudice.

It was beyond embarrassing, but typical of the Brit Lit mainstream in action. No point writing to the broadsheet newspaper. Their arts editor would have commissioned the fucking thing in the first place. But I sent a letter off to Tillie immediately c/o her hotel in London. I knew where she was staying. Mary Gray Hughes had written me with the information in advance of her trip. My letter made her laugh and cheered her up no end. I didn't keep a copy of the letter. It must have been my anger that cheered her up.

Following the bookfair event that day in San Francisco I spent a couple of days in Tillie's company. Although into her eighties she remained politically active within her own community, and lived in the same cooperative housing project that she had since the end of the Second World War, and in the same apartment. But it was a big roomy apartment, stowed out with books; neat as I remember. Tillie was a widow. Her husband had been a longshoreman, a docker as we would say in Glasgow.

The housing project had been formed by a mix of longshoremen, trades unionists, African Americans and Japanese immigrants. It was a treat to walk with her about the area, enjoying the number of friends who waved her over for a chat. This gave me a little more knowledge of the San Francisco radical tradition and how it operated within communities as well as in literary circles and those of political activists. She was then immersed in a campaign on behalf of the libraries in San

Francisco. She invited me to a radical church meeting the coming Sunday. It didn't matter whether you had any religion at all never mind which one. It was just a glad-to-be-alive engagement for anybody who wanted to go, especially those who enjoyed music. And the music was brilliant, a rhythm and blues band and chorus, led by a male lead vocalist.

Twenty years later, in 2007, I was preparing to leave for San José for a six-month job at the State University. I emailed a friend whom I thought would know if Tillie was still around. She was still around. Then the day before I left I received a second email: Tillie had died two days previously, she was 94 years of age.

An Artist lives in Scotland

An Artist lives in Scotland[1]

Between Hunterston Terminal and Portencross in Ayrshire runs a track by the beach and here beneath a cliff is located an isolated cottage known locally as Northbank. This is where the artist Alasdair Taylor lived and worked for forty years. He moved there back in 1965 with his wife and two daughters. His wife died several years before him and thereon Taylor lived alone. In 2005 he suffered a major stroke. He showed tremendous tenacity and courage in the fight to survive but suffered a degree of paralysis, including the loss of the use of his right hand. He had to leave Northbank Cottage. There was no choice.

It was a particularly trying period for his family. Taylor was an experienced and skilled keeper of art. His cottage with its dilapidated outbuildings were crammed full of paintings, sculpture, painted stone, his 'found' works. It was a magnificent collection, the product of a lifetime's commitment to his art. Then on top of that or side by side with that, underneath and over above, were the artefacts and ephemera, the tools and equipage; the notebooks, papers and old correspondence, the books: all manner of stuff, everything, everywhere you looked, collected by this working artist over a period of fifty years. What would happen to it? The proceeds of the sale would be swallowed up in the purchase of a place that allowed him to cope with this physical, fundamental change to his life and circumstances. But what about his work and all the stuff?

There was also the immediate worry, if some catastrophic calamity befell the cottage during his long period of recovery in hospital. What then? What was to happen? It was a logistical nightmare. Wherever he was to end up, could the collection travel with him? Could it be stored? How would it be done?

Alasdair Gray was a close friend of the family. He and Taylor had been friends since their time at Glasgow School of Art. In early March of that year I drove with him down to Portencross, along with the artist Euan Sutherland and Malcolm Dickson, Director of Street Level Gallery. Taylor's daughter Jean was present to open the cottage for us. The first step was to obtain a clearer idea of what existed. This meant going through everything, piece by piece, picture by picture. Malcolm and Euan worked their way through it, assisted by Alasdair Gray.

I wandered around. The collection was breathtaking. I had known Taylor's work for twenty years but wasn't prepared for this. In years past I was fortunate to see his work in three private exhibitions. More to the point I had visited here at Northbank on several occasions, especially during 1986. I was then operating as a 'man with a van'. I had got dough from somewhere and used it to buy an elderly transit (1600cc). A good joiner I knew customised the interior. This meant I could strap down paintings and large mirrors. I called the business Art Moves and specialised in the transportation of artworks. I was helped on occasion by a friend who worked full-time as a picture-framer but fancied moving out on his own one day.[2]

The biggest job I had was through Alasdair Gray: the transportation of the Five Artists Exhibition. Gray organised and financed the exhibition almost wholly on his own. It was a mammoth exhibition. Through this I also got to know Carole Gibbons and John Connolly. The fifth artist of the group was Alan Fletcher who had died tragically many years before.

A few months later Art Moves came to an abrupt end. I was passing through Paisley on my way home from a job; I had just delivered a painting, when I noticed smoke from under the bonnet. I stopped and jumped out: the engine was on fire. The van burnt down. That was the end of Art Moves.

This visit in March 2005 was my first for a long while. North-bank Cottage is located a hundred yards from the shore, overlooking the north coast of Arran, the Sound of Bute and Little Cumbrae. I was reminded of a previous visit, sitting at the living room window staring out, aware of the moment by moment shift in light, sound and movement, of sea and sky, of land, vegetation, even the air itself, the sense that there is only movement, there is nothing but movement. Labels like 'abstract expressionism' become not so much meaningless as a route to misunderstanding. They subvert the insight required to appreciate what it is the artist is doing, the enormity of the task, the extent of the achievement. Alasdair Taylor's art may carry the label 'abstract expressionism' but what value does such a label carry? When I was sitting in the artist's living room looking out the window it occurred to me that in Taylor's art we find the most intense realism. In some of those wild paintings it is as though the artist has trapped the very elements. What are 'the very elements'? Movement; only movement.

In 2005 I had the daydream that Northbank Cottage and its outbuildings might have been transformed into a space for a permanent exhibition of this artist's work. There are different ways to view a work of art. A single painting can be hung on your living-room wall or in a gallery surrounded by the work of other artists. The work of one artist may be collected in a permanent exhibition in a space devoted solely to it, charting different periods in the artist's development. For those who doubt the merit of an artist's middle or later work it can be instrumental to see what he or she was producing at an earlier stage.

To see the artist's own work in its own location is rare. In some permanent spaces the curator will try to recreate this, exhibiting personal and found objects, not to enhance the finished work but to offer another dimension. For a limited period during Taylor's hospitalization, Northbank Cottage was as it was when he lived and worked there. The art was there for the taking. There is no doubt that money could have been found to house a permanent site through the combined effort of local and national authorities.

Major art is a major attraction, not only for tourists from overseas but tourists from Scotland, people who want to see what their artists are up to. The preferred site would have been in North Ayrshire. Let people see Taylor's work in the context of that glorious coastline, and throughout the four seasons; once they experience the local weather.

In other parts of the world permanent exhibitions are devoted to the work of individual artists. Scotland has very few of these. Those with the authority to arrange it lack the will, capacity and/or confidence to make a judgment. They seem unable to work out if the value of a piece of art only holds within a Scottish context. Let us ship Alasdair Taylor's collection to New York City and put the question to an American critic: Please sir, is this the work of a real artist or just a Scottish one?

A fundamental distinction between artists and bureaucrats is the will to judge. Artists make judgments constantly, intuitive and otherwise. No decent bureaucrat arrives at an answer through that process. Any good bureaucrat avoids judgments, and avoids the intuitive form at all costs. They need a decision-procedure, where an end statement is arrived at step-by-step, by logical inference. In this way no one can be accused of making a decision. The difficulty with great art is that it moves by its own accord, if and where necessary.

By seventy years of age Alasdair Taylor had never received one penny from the public purse to support and sustain his art. No public money was ever spent on its appearance in public gallery exhibitions. None was ever spent on the acquisition of one solitary sculpture or painting. This is not because he would have declined such offers. None was ever made. And that alone would have counted against him. Who within the arts bureaucracy has the confidence to admit that a man ignored for a lifetime may be a major Scottish artist?

Of those who were familiar with his name a minority might have seen his work in private exhibitions, notably the Five Artists Show. None of the artists had any money at all apart from Alasdair Gray, who funded the project from the cash he earned from his novel Lanark. He finished close to bankruptcy when the Scottish Arts Council's panel of experts, to their shame, rejected his request for support to offset financial loss. They were "particularly concerned about the basic concept of the exhibition."[3]

Some may recognise Alasdair Taylor from Gray's *Portrait of a Painter*, published in Lean Tales, 1985. Unfortunately this brave and exciting essay failed to entice any Scottish arts authorities into making the journey to North Ayrshire. This must baffle people unattuned to cultural life in this country. Surely they read Gray's essay? Who knows. Nobody made the journey. Gray is one of a band of artists whose work is known, respected and even loved in other parts of the world yet his advocacy failed to move the arts establishment.

Gray's essay is more than the portrait of an artist: it offers the possibility of a Scottish art criticism unafraid to acknowledge greatness in a living Scottish artist where the merit of the artist has not firstly been argued and established beyond the Scottish borders, by foreign critics or commentators.

An originality of vision is required to acknowledge artistic merit in any new work; beside boldness and imagination the critic must take a risk. Scotland is in dire need of good critics, especially those unafraid to go public. Their absence leaves the way clear for third-rate commentary. I come across the literary side more than any other. Consistent in the attacks on contemporary literature is a general lack of understanding of the nature of art and its creation, and a peculiar naivety. Few show any grasp of the formal problems that have faced Scottish writers during the past two and a half centuries.

At the public level where such media commentators operate, ignorance is no excuse. It springs from a less edifying feature of the Scottish Enlightenment: the drive to root out Scotticisms; a fear of the 'uncouth' indigenous, whether in manners, customs or language. There was an excuse in the Eighteenth Century. Nowadays we may see it for what it is: a pathetic mixture of cynicism and cowardice.

The way I saw it the situation faced by Alasdair Taylor is the extent to which Scottish society values its own culture. The neglect of an artist such as Alasdair Taylor borders on the wilful. It contaminates our culture and represents a humiliation for those artists who receive or have received support from the public purse, and I am one of them. Taylor never. The neglect casts doubt on the legitimacy of the salaries received by employees of the Arts Council and of arts-funded formations like the Scottish Book Trust, the Saltire Society, and public art galleries, libraries and museums; in fact any body or institution funded to advance or support the art and culture of this country.

I support the existence of a body funded by public money that acts on behalf of the Scottish public in support of its art and artists. This may never have been a description of the Scottish Arts Council. Perhaps it could in the future. Individuals within such a body would be capable of making decisions independently, based on the judgments of artists and critics knowledgeable of art in Scotland as well as art in general. The trick is to acknowledge the work of artists who are not yet dead. Don't leave it to the current department of tourism whose relationship to art will be akin to that of the DSS – the Department of Social Security – toward truth and social justice. The creation of art is not a cottage industry.

Back at Northbank Cottage in 2005 Malcolm Dickson and Euan Sutherland discussed with Alasdair Gray and Jean Taylor the basic requirements to safeguard her father's collection. In the first instance a photographer would document everything within the cottage, outbuildings and surrounding habitat. Then the cataloguing and packaging of each painting and sculpture would take place; and a proper assessment of the 'found' objects, plus anything else that was to be retained. The plant hire included wooden pallets and two portacabins for storage and transportation; additional costs included insurance and further storage. Labour costs would be kept to the minimum. The initial work might be carried out within a three to four week period. A basic estimate of £5,000 was proposed to the Scottish

Arts Council and this was allocated, thus the collection was catalogued and digitised and for that, for some reason, I feel grateful, which appears to sum up Scotland.

Anyway, none of us live forever and Taylor was a practical man. Even while hospitalized he was training himself in the use of his left hand. It is good to report that in 2007 a small retrospective exhibition of his work did happen, at the Harbour Arts Centre, Irvine. He died the same year. A small posthumous exhibition of his work took place a year later, alongside his friend and comrade, Alasdair Gray.[4] The rest is silence, as far as I know.

Hugh Savage and the
Workers City tradition

The first I remember meeting with Hugh Savage was on a picket line in January 1990. This was the first month of Glasgow's reign as European City of Culture and this the City's premier cultural product. The phrase 'cultural product' indicates the value placed by the Labour Council on the city's cultural heritage and tradition which was no value at all other than as a business commodity; and to what extent its parts might be sold to tourists and visitors. And already Workers City was on the attack. Hugh Savage, Leslie Forster and Ned Donaldson, friends for fifty years, alongside Isabel and Freddie Anderson, Farquhar McLay and Jeanette McGinn, widow of the late Matt McGinn.

Other friends and acquaintances were present, most long-standing activists. Some were ex-members of political parties; some remained members of political parties and others had never been that way inclined. Present in abundance were experience and energy both physical and intellectual. Individuals held and expressed different opinions. In common was a left-wing sensibility, an impatience with humbug and a distrust of professional politicians and arts administrators.

Workers City was a non-sectarian formation and did its best to remain that way. The group's critique of the 1990 European City of Culture produced an outlandish response from the political authorities, a little of the same from the arts establishment. There was an ambiguity within the mainstream media: on the whole they approved, this because any enemy of the Labour Party is an ally. What angered the political authorities most was their inability to control or put an end to the public debate. What on earth was happening here? How come nobody was putting a stop to it! And what about that scandal-mongering organ, The Glasgow Keelie, produced anonymously, distributed freely. Had the political machinery failed? Where the hell were the media! Surely it was their job to control debate?

The authorities were unable to grasp that what goes on in ordinary life, where people talk among themselves freely, is natural human behaviour.

In Scotland, the name 'keelie' has been applied pejoratively to Glaswegians for decades. The dictionary I have defines 'keelie' as 'street-arab' and 'pickpocket' but when applied generally 'keelie' denotes 'low class', 'vulgar beings', 'the great unwashed', etc. The Workers City group applied it to themselves after the fashion of African-American activists using the term 'nigger', and the 'Keelie became its heart.

The appearance of this free newspaper coincided with particular campaigns and demonstrations. Its primary targets were Labour politicians at local and national level, and where possible it named names and used photographs. It featured snippets of local history and lampoons in the form of poetry or cartoons. Everyone associated with Workers City was encouraged to contribute.

The Labour authorities knew they were in a fight and along the way they suffered some defeats. The most notable was their bungled attempt to sell a third of Glasgow Green to private developers. They were unprepared for the depth of revulsion felt by Glaswegians and completely underestimated the opposition. This mistake derives from a failing common to mainstream politicians: ignorance. They fail to grasp that a world exists beyond their own sphere of involvement, and in this other world forms of politics also exist. Ironically, the sharpest lesson drawn was how little Labour Party politicians knew of the origins of their own party; of Labour history itself they knew next to nothing, and cared even less. If they had they would have approached with caution the Workers City group whose campaigns hijacked the front page of the local newspapers on several occasions, and made the news in Australia as well as New York City.

Workers City rarely featured more than fifteen or twenty individuals but received strong outside support and solidarity. It had no leaders in point of principle but Hugh Savage was pivotal. It is difficult to overstate the respect others held for him.

Until then, the late 1980s, his main involvement had been with the Friends of the People's Palace, a group of volunteers who came together to support and raise funds for the People's Palace museum on Glasgow Green. Money raised by the 'Friends' went from assisting in the purchase of historical relics and art objects to buying a photocopying machine for the museum office, which indicates the appalling lack of resources endured by staff.

Hugh Savage's relationship to the museum was an important factor in the Workers City campaigns. The museum's curator Elspeth King and her assistant Michael Donnelly had transformed the old place into something quite special; a proper people's museum whose existence gave the lie to the politicians' fantasy of Clydeside as historical home to budding billionaires and global entrepreneurs, following in the wake of the 18th century businessmen who made their fortunes through trafficking in the enslavement and exploitation of human beings. Elspeth King and Michael Donnelly knew radical history and treasured it, literally, on behalf of the people of Glasgow. For Hugh Savage this was primary. Radical history and tradition were fundamental to the spirit of Workers City. His close friends Leslie Forster and Ned Donaldson had been involved in the Labour Movement all their working lives. Similarly, of other comrades on that first picket line, Farquhar Mclay, Freddie and Isabel Anderson, Janette McGinn were students as well as keepers of radical history.

Thus the Labour-controlled Council authorities wanted rid of them. They wanted outsiders, preferably people with no knowledge of the city's radical past, with no personal attachment. They wanted people who would grasp the nettle, understand the concept 'paid employee', and do the council's bidding at any cost. By all means allow a place for working-class culture but not on its own terms. Forget Willie Nairn, John Maclean, Harry McShane, Guy Aldred, bring on Harry Lauder, the cast of Still Game, Billy Connolly, Oor Wullie and the Broons.

What about disease-ridden slums, state repression, police brutality, rent strikes and racism; sectarianism, the struggle for adequate living conditions; a proper life for our children? Forget it, not unless there is a happy ending. Tourists prefer to exit 'cultural outlets' (art galleries, theatres and museums) with a smile on their face. Why would financiers, Captains of Industry and super entrepreneurs wish to know about militant suffragettes, Marxists, socialists, anarchists, communists and all manner of antiparliamentarians. They especially didn't need reminding by a few pensioners and a bunch of leftie oddballs.

This manipulation of the city's history was at the core of the critique offered by the group that became known as Workers City. Even the location of the People's Palace was a problem for the Labour Council. It was the Calton. This old inner city district is in its own right famous, or notorious, depending on your politics. In 1787 there was a demonstration by the Calton weavers there in Abercromby Street. The British troops shot dead seven of them, seven men on a demonstration. They were buried in the nearest cemetery. In the 1930s Harry McShane campaigned to raise funds for a memorial stone laid for the seven. Sixty years later his old friend and comrade Hugh Savage, supported by the Friends of the People's Palace and the Workers City group, raised funds for a new one. This was erected on the same spot, close to where the outrage took place.

Hugh Savage was born and bred in the Calton. As late as 2005, fifteen years after the Labour authorities spent £50 million on the 'European City of Culture' jamboree, the life expectancy of males in this district was less than 54 years of age. It requires repeating: the life expectancy of males in the Calton was 54 years of age in 2005. For the United Kingdom as a whole the life expectancy of males in the same year was 75.9 years. For the upper classes it was 98.6 years and that was for the corgi dogs. Glasgow people are used to their politicians being embarrassed by such statistics rather than outraged. The very existence of the People's Palace was a reminder of the stark reality and the radical working-class tradition. If it could have been uprooted and set down in the vicinity of middle-class Bearsden the authorities would have tried for that.

They solved the problem by removing the museum's curator and her assistant. They began by denigrating the work of the assistant then sacking him. Then they tried to force the curator's resignation by humiliating her publicly. That failed. So they applied the new right-wing tactic of forcing difficult employees to reapply for their own job, then giving it to somebody else. That succeeded, but not without a struggle. The Workers City group campaigned on her behalf and Hugh

Savage was to the fore, bringing with him the Friends of the People's Palace. And the citizens of Glasgow rallied in support.

News of the treachery of the Labour Party in Glasgow and the campaign reached the Australian media. Who ever heard of such a thing? A public campaign to save the job of a museum curator? More letters reached Glasgow's Herald newspaper than for any news event since the evangelist Billy Graham's tour in the 1950s. Finally the authorities succeeded in forcing Elspeth out altogether. They gave her job to a young man from the north of Ireland whom she had helped train in the first place.

Following the end of 'Culture Year' the activities of the Workers City group wound down but people stayed in touch with one another. For a period Hugh Savage and a few others continued to publish The Glasgow Keelie. Some became involved in the struggle against industrial and environmental disease with Clydeside Action on Asbestos. Then, to most everybody's surprise, Hugh Savage flitted from the east end of Glasgow to Rothesay on the island of Bute.

But two or three days a week he travelled into the city's Mitchell Library to meet with Forster and Donaldson, and other friends too. This trio were members of the Glasgow Labour History Workshop. Radical history and political affairs, whether historical or contemporary; those were passions. As young men they had been encouraged by Harry McShane and his belief in the power of radical history. They worked on projects before, during and after the time of Workers City.

Hugh and Leslie published All for the Cause, a book on Willie Nairn, 'Stonebreaker, Philosopher, Marxist'. They were prominent in the publication of The Singer Strike Clydebank, 1911; Militant Workers: Labour and Class Conflict on the Clyde 1900–1950; Roots of Red Clydeside 1910–1914; Labour Unrest and Industrial Relations in West Scotland.

Forster published his own memoir, Rocking the Boat,[1] and with Ned Donaldson wrote Sell and be Damned, The Glasgow Merrylee Housing Scandal of 1951.[2] The work they did into their seventies is inspirational, packed full of information: to read them is to come into contact with a roll-call of outstanding men and women. They were more excited by the unknown or forgotten names, "the unsung heroes who toiled to enlighten the workers without any thought of gain other than the spreading of the word of Marx and Engels."

For all that Hugh Savage was an activist first, and the writing came down the list. Beside the research, there were angry letters to the powers-that-be. Such writing is done for immediate use and not much of Hugh's output remains but some does, and featured in the Addenda to his Born Up a Close: Memoirs of a Brigton Boy,[3] including his contributions to campaigning features from earlier times, published in Socialist Revolt and New Commune, two radical journals that he and his friends and comrades produced back in the 1950s.

It is unclear when he began on his 'memoirs'. It was not something he discussed easily. When he saw reviews for the publication of another 'life of an old socialist' he gave a shake of the head, sadly: Not another one . . . He considered such projects an embarrassing aspect of the ageing process. Now here he was doing the same thing. He described himself as 'a foot-soldier' and worried about being presumptuous. His family and friends encouraged him and he stuck to the task.

When he moved to the place in Rothesay he did most of the heavy graft himself. He gutted the place and put in a new central heating system which meant boring through the sandstone wall of the tenement building. Then he redecorated completely, renovating all the plasterwork, the lot. Hugh was a plumber and welder to trade and had always been a fit active man, a teetotaller and nonsmoker. But he was then into his seventies. When did he find time to get on with his writing? In fact he didn't hardly at all. I asked him and he nodded, he was trying. He had begun to experience acute back pain, it was impossible to stay at the keyboard for long.

The stress he suffered from that move to Rothesay was not only physical. The political atmosphere on the island he found stultifying and anachronistic. He was not joking entirely when he said the Masonic Lodge controlled anything not already controlled by the Marquis of Bute. He saw religious sectarianism dividing a community still in thrall to the local aristocracy. This in the 1990s. Everybody living in the place was having to pay the aristocracy ground rent. The Marquis was a feudal lord, and cousin to the British monarchy. This side of Rothesay, bound in with sectarianism and obeisance to the aristocracy took the form of a shameful family secret for Hugh, not only an indictment of Scottish society but an embarrassment. If an injustice was afoot it would prey on his mind and he barely could discuss the subject.

Except nobody was doing anything, they were just taking the punishment. That was the worst of it. Nobody was fighting back, or seemed to be. He heard of a battle being waged against two of his elderly neighbours by the factors of the Marquis. The issue concerned a drainage and sewage problem. He took up the cudgels alongside his neighbours, and got sucked into that mire of civil disputation which can masquerade as politics in Scotland.

At the same time he was tackling the authorities on his own behalf with his continued refusal to pay the Poll Tax. Every skirmish meant wasted time and energy composing letters to the authorities, re Jarndyce & Jarndyce, begging your Lordship's leave. One such skirmish led to his appearance at the High Court in Glasgow. It was over his refusal to have his name entered onto the Electoral Roll. He refused to pay all or any part of the fines levied against him and was prepared to do a couple of months in jail if so required. When he was called to the dock he bewildered the court by addressing them on the theme of 'freedom'. Who was this old man, this ghost of the radical past . . . People looked askance, then lowered their gaze, only raising their head when he finished talking. No comment, no throat-clearing, no furtive glances. A couple of seconds of a pause, the case was dismissed; back to normal, begging your Lordship's pardon. Hugh was out the door by then.

I hoped he might return to his memoir but life kept getting in the way. He was not especially perturbed. He had taken it beyond boyhood, early manhood and the start of the 2nd World War. He was satisfied with that.

This was the period he began work on Clydeside, joined the CPGB, became a labour activist, militant trade unionist, got married, started a family. In the Party he had a growing reputation but the 2nd World War and shifts in policy was a grave problem for committed young activists. His "first political activity as a new Communist was advancing the call for a People's Peace, with negotiations with Germany and Hitler." Unfortunately most men around the Clyde shipyards – including Communist Party members – had relations, friends or acquaintances in the armed forces. Some had suffered bereavement. Now the Party was as good as telling them it was in vain and Hugh occasionally "had to dodge when a heavy spanner was flung at [his] head." Ironically, had this policy not then been in operation one of the turning points on Clydeside would not have occurred: the great Apprentices Strike of 1941. Moscow's opposition to the war at that particular period allowed the CPGB membership to support the striking apprentices.

This was the strike that shut down the Clyde shipyards. Hugh downplayed his own part. He was not then an apprentice but a young journeyman plumber and welder, and his role was governed by that. But there is no question that he was involved centrally. He was twenty-three at the time; close to the apprentices and pals with a few, including young Communists like Johnny Muir, a strike leader. Strategical matters were the business of the apprentices' own strike committee and Hugh was very clear on that point.

Yet his own involvement was highlighted by the shameful actions of the British State. Acting on behalf of the shipyard owners, Hugh and Johnnie Moore were served with their call-up papers, and destined for the front line. It made no difference that they worked in a prescribed industry. This had happened to other militant workers when employers wanted rid of them. The political authorities were as attentive to the demands of big business then as they are now. Hugh had little doubt that he and Moore would have been killed had older and more experienced trade unionists not challenged the authorities on their behalf:

Fifty odd years have passed since that incident but I can still recall that at that period in the war the Royal Marines were going through a particularly bad spell with land assaults being launched from places like Crete and they were having very heavy casualties. Now I knew how vicious and mean the capitalist class could be and was quickly learning what governments and the establishment have in store for anyone who dares to challenge their authority. But really the authorities had been very stupid, they could just have staggered the call-ups and made sure we went to different regiments. In my own case I would not have known, being politically quite immature. I really did not suspect a thing if it had not been for the others, maybe especially when I saw the determination on Bob McLennan's face that morning and then when he said to us "The bastards are not going to murder any workers from John Brown's."

After the war he was blacklisted by the shipyards, and much of the building industry. 1948 proved a crucial year for him. It began with the resignation of George 'Geordie' Buchanan, MP for Glasgow Gorbals who had held the seat for twenty years. Buchanan was a close friend of James Maxton, John Wheatley, Campbell Stephen and the early ILPers, as they were known. In those days the ILP (Independent Labour Party) was affiliated to the Labour Party.

A little digging into radical history reveals Buchanan to have been one of the original Red Clydesiders who stormed the Westminster barricades in the 1922 General Election. One of his contenders for the seat was John Maclean. Maclean had advised the Gorbals electorate that if they didn't vote for him they should vote for Geordie Buchanan. It was Maclean's last campaign. He died a year later. Before Buchanan the seat had been held by George Barnes. Barnes won it back in 1906 on behalf of the Labour Representation Committee and Keir Hardie was there in his support. During that forty-two year period Barnes and Buchanan were the only two MPs to occupy the seat. Even then, Buchanan only resigned to accept promotion to a junior ministerial position under Tom Johnston, then

Secretary of State for Scotland. This was why the by-election had been called.

The CPGB decided to fight the seat and offered Hugh Savage temporary work as full-time election agent. He gave up his trade and took on the job. It was the only occasion in his political life that he accepted paid employment as a Communist Party official. The Communist Party member whom the hierarchy selected as candidate was Peter Kerrigan. Hugh Savage became his election agent. In that capacity he was often in Gorbals and there met with Harry McShane, then living in a room and kitchen flat attached to the local Party office. McShane was known nationally and had been since the 1920s. Within socialist circles he had been known as an activist for much longer than that. Until making McShane's acquaintance Hugh Savage described himself as "a good wee Stalinist." It is no exaggeration to say that the course of his life now altered. A friendship developed that lasted all of forty years, right until McShane's death at the age of ninety-six.

In the immediate post-war years living conditions were horrendous in working-class Glasgow and municipal housing was a necessary area of engagement for activists. And also necessary for the city's MPs and councillors to show interest in the issue, as an election promise if nothing more. John Wheatley had set the standard in the preceding decade with his work in the area. After Wheatley's death Geordie Buchanan continued the ILP tradition and "was especially active in initiating the drive against slum housing . . ." Within the Communist

114

Party Harry McShane made it a priority, and it became so too for younger comrades. In the 1940s James McLaren and Hugh Savage formed housing associations in Brigton and Calton districts. In 1951, Forster and Donaldson led a major campaign against Glasgow City Council and the executive's incredible attempt to sell off its new council housing stock in the high-amenity district of Merrylee.

In 1950 Hugh Savage was nominated the CPGB candidate for Dalmarnock in the city's municipal elections. Soon after-wards, he, Leslie Forster, Ned Donaldson, Matt McGinn, Bill McCulloch and Harry McShane resigned from the Commu-nist Party. In his memoir Rocking the Boat, Leslie Forster refers to one significant incident that occurred during

> a keynote speech made by Bill Lauchlan, the Scottish Secretary . . . at a Scottish Congress of the CP held in Glas-gow. When he finished his peroration, delegates stood up clapping again and again in praise of the Messiah. During this display of adoration Ned Donaldson and Hugh Savage remained seated . . .

Hugh was a reader and he had a love for performance art-forms like music and drama, and a fondness for show-business and show-business characters. The singer and comedian Glen Daly was his close friend from their time together on Clydeside. Hugh typically referred to him by his real name, Bartholomew Francis Dick.

Anecdotes concern people and Hugh enjoyed hearing them or narrating them. On that picket-line the first time I spoke with him, a young English journalist arrived from a southern broadsheet who wanted to know who exactly was involved. Hugh shrugged: We're all Keelies here son, he said.

Friendship and loyalty were the crucial qualities. He was a powerful campaigner. He took care to know what was what, and how far he could go. I remember the police attempting to move him and a couple of others from a pavement where they were selling copies of the 'Keelie. Hugh just looked at them. Oh naw son, this is a public walkway. The police discussed it among themselves, then one attempted to defend themselves by advising Hugh that his dad was a trade unionist.

He was a boxer as a boy, and always a fighter, and usually he knew how far to go. He was known for his 'strong tongue' and it was better not getting on the end of it. A newspaper carried a report on a confrontation the City administration had suffered with Workers City; the headline read 'Savaged'. He enjoyed telling us how the exact same was once said of his father after a fight down the 'Booly', behind Brigton Cross: "Savage by name and Savage by nature."

His other close friend was a Rottweiler dog by the name of Rory. Even for a Rottweiler Rory was big. Hugh had trained Rory to be suspicious of anybody wearing a suit. That helped when Poll Tax officers and other authority figures came unannounced to the door.

Rory was prone to jealousy. If anybody looked twice at his pal one of those deep gurgling growls came from the dog's throat. It was a distinctive gurgle, like the last drops of some poor guy's blood being swirled about. On one occasion during the Workers City days the 'Keelie was targetting suspected political corruption in a Glasgow district. It was rumoured that a few heavies were going to disrupt one of the editorial meetings and sort everybody out. Hugh shrugged. When the night arrived he brought his pal, Rory. When the heavy squad arrived we were to let them in, then shut the door and let loose the dog. On the night none of the heavy squad turned up so who knows what would have happened.

On occasion one had to travel as a passenger in Hugh's car; humans at the front, Rottweilers to the rear, and the harsh breathing, that tongue lolling a few inches from the back of your neck. If forced to speak you tried to do so without moving your jaw. Hugh's method of restraining the dog was to call at him and grasp him by the neck. He was a strong man but over seventy at the time; there was an outside chance he might be unable to restrain Rory's almighty lungings.

Like his close friend Leslie Forster, Hugh's conversation was crammed full of names. Their knowledge has been inspirational for myself. My original aim in the introduction to his memoirs was to supply additional detail to the political context in footnotes, and a bibliography that contained books and pamphlets relating to local radical history, in the hope people might want to explore and discover more.

The footnotes became lengthier. Each name mentioned by Hugh may be likened to a computerized 'suitcase-folder': double-click and up comes a series of folders, each one of which contains documents, references and biographical detail that in turn lead to other folders.

The books in the bibliography come from my own library; most of which I have picked up along the way. My library has enlarged through the inclusion of some that belonged to others, including a few from Hugh, and through him and Leslie Forster a few also from the library of James McLaren who died from tuberculosis back in 1947, still in his twenties.[4] Had McLaren lived he surely would have moved in the same intellectual direction as his friends, in increasing opposition to the line issued by the Party and, ultimately, to resign from it.

Hugh wanted a title for his memoirs that would detract from the idea that he himself was of any importance and suggested 'Born Up a Close' for that very reason. Les Forster disagreed and chose a quotation from Thomas Paine, and Tommy Gorman agreed. Perhaps Hugh's children, Laureen and Scott also agreed but were too considerate of my feelings to tell me!

But Hugh could not have been clearer to me about the matter. It nagged at him that he was writing such a thing at all. His life was no more worthy than anybody else; that was the way he saw it, describing himself as a 'foot-soldier'. Sometimes he was reluctant to discuss the project. At rare times it excited him. He had little interest in his own feelings, at least not in print. There wasn't an ounce of sentimentality in the man. He was able to admit, eventually, that his account of his early years was never to do with his own importance, it was for the historical record. Only the information is crucial, part of our radical history here on Clydeside.

The Voice of Amos Tutuola[1]

In 1970, by a fluke, I obtained the second edition of John Francis Campbell's Popular Tales of the West Highlands. I have been reading them ever since. This beautiful work was transcribed from the Gàidhlig by collectors in mid-nineteenth century Scotland. The stories were narrated to them by people in the West Highlands and islands, and translated by Campbell himself. The collection is published in four volumes. Without his English translations it would have been impossible for me to read them. I never learned Gàidhlig. It was the first language of my paternal grandmother but none of her children, never mind myself and my brothers, ever had it bequeathed. She sang to us in Gàidhlig, laughed at us in Gàidhlig, and spoke to us in English.

J. F. Campbell had been instructed by the then Duke of Argyll that he should publish the stories in the English translation only. To his great credit he did not abide by the imperious command. He used a team of collectors of whom John Dewar was central. Dewar himself was chief component of Campbell's 'collecting machine' which is how J. F. described him. Dewar earned a living as best he could and in 1860 was "working as a labourer in the woods at Rosneath," only fifty miles from Glasgow. In those days people in the area spoke Gàidhlig.

The woods hereabouts are located at the head of the peninsula and I am quite familiar with the place myself, having once owned a caravan at the local caravan site. Submarine commanders are also familiar with the area, as are sailors and other security personnel of Her Majesty's Armed Forces. It's a mile's sail from where the USA have kept nuclear warheads and missiles on a form of military alert since the early 1960s. They don't need any street lights around these parts. Everything and everybody glow in the dark according to the locals, not just the fish and the misshapen, strangely proportioned shellfish. The locals make it a boast that if anything goes seriously wrong in the world they'll be first to go.

This British aristocrat, the Duke of Argyll, owned the woods and most if not all of the Rosneath peninsula. This was one tiny portion of the family's very extensive land holdings and properties. For all I know they still own it. It sickens me to read that kind of stuff. J. F. Campbell had a family connection to the Duke so they weren't all loathsome. Here is a brief extract from *The Story of Conall Gulban*, one of the tales collected by John Dewar, translated by J. F. Campbell:

> She seized me then in her talons; she sailed to the back of the ocean with me; and she sprang to the clouds with me, and I was a while that I did not know which was heaven or earth for me, nor whether she would let me fall in the

drowning sea, or on rocks of hardness, or on cairns of stones; she was lifting me and letting me down, till she saw that I was soon dead, on the breast of the sea. Though I was not heavy, when I took the brine I was heavy indeed; and when she was lifting me she was spent.

Of the other two versions of this story one was from Hector Maclean of Isla, another of J. F. Campbell's collectors. The second version was collected by John McNair, a shoemaker from Dunoon. McNair got the story from another shoemaker back in 1809, an old man from Glendaruel by the name of Duncan Livingston. This old storyteller had a reputation. It was said of him that

at the time of the American war [of Independence], the laird was pressing the tenants to go, and [he] seemed not willing; so they pursued him through a deep river, or burn, as we call it; and when he saw he could not escape, he placed his leg between two stones and snapped it in two, so they had to carry him home.

John Dewar got stories from the same source, passed down by the grandson of Duncan Livingston. According to Dewar *The Story of Conall Gulban* dates back several centuries to the Christian Crusades and the invasion of Turkey. Variations of the story were told throughout Scotland. J. F. Campbell said he heard the same story from "Irish labourers in London."

A most interesting aspect of this is the incidental information that one of the Irishmen, "a bricklayer", read the story in manuscript. In recent times the British authorities had denied Gàidhlig was ever a written language at all. Occasionally this disinformation surfaces in the form of rhetoric: schoolchildren and listeners to BBC Radio programmes are asked to answer the question: Is Gaelic a language?

There is nothing new nor unique in that. The exclusion and inferiorization of indigenous languages and traditions are primary aspects of imperialism. The intellectual colonization of Scottish life and culture has been around for several hundred years.

I discovered the J. F. Campbell collections in the early 1970s and towards the end of the same decade I came upon the work of Amos Tutuola; this from The Palm-Wine Drinkard (1952):

They were very pleased as my wife was dancing with them, but when my wife felt tired, these creatures were not tired, then my wife stopped, and when they saw her all of them were greatly annoyed and dragged her to continue with them and when she started again, she became tired before them, so she stopped as before, then they came to her and said that she must dance until she should be released. But as she was dancing again and I saw that she was exceedingly tired and these creatures did not stop at all, then I went to her and said to her 'let us go,' but as she was following me, these creatures grew annoyed with me. They wanted to take her back to the dance from me by force. So I performed my juju there again, and it changed my wife into the wooden-doll as usual, then I put it into my pocket, and they saw her no more. (p116)

I looked again at *The Story of Conall Gulban*, the extract above beginning "She seized me then in her talons; she sailed to the back of the ocean with me . . ." One thing seemed clear, that the Nigerian writer of the wonderful The Palm-Wine Drinkard would not only enjoy these translated Gàidhlig tales from the West Highlands and islands of Scotland, but would have felt an affinity. I felt a kinship with Amos Tutuola, and it was immediate, as soon as I entered his world.

It certainly would have interested myself to see the manuscript read to J. F. Campbell by 'the Irish bricklayer'; not the subject matter but the 'speaking voice', the 'voice' of the narrator.

And what is the *value* of the phrase 'the Irish bricklayer'. What is implicit? What do we infer about this man?

Also in the 1970s I read Sam Selvon's The Lonely Londoners (1956) and experienced a similar literary kinship. I was then in my twenties, with one published collection of stories. I enjoyed the company of other writers; colleagues and peers. Tutuola and Selvon were of my father's generation. Nevertheless I would have enjoyed sitting down over a beer, exchanging ideas and thoughts on racism, elitism, colonization; linguistic imperialism and the art and craft of writing, and maybe have a laugh, sharing anecdotes on the literary establishment's opinion of 'rotten English', in the words of another Nigerian writer, Ken Saro-Wiwa.

Language itself is the issue, the means to self-expression, and the need to find a way into and through the writing process that might allow the story to breathe and bring to life our characters. Not any story but our own stories individually, stories from our own communities. In common we had language. Not any language but a language thrust upon us; an imperial language that had colonized just about every area of our existence: Standard English literary form.

The imposition of this linguistic arsenal, this so-called 'literary language', acted to kill our stories stone-dead. That was how I saw it and how I related to the work of these Caribbean and African writers. This solidarity was in direct opposition to what I felt towards writers who were content to accept the Standard English literary form as it was thrust upon them, making from it whatever they could. These writers did not have to belong to the English or British upper-classes, they could be Indian, African, Irish, American, South East Asian. Writers who accepted Standard English literary form were prostrating themselves, their community, their traditions. Yes, these forms of assimilation are thrust upon us, but none has to take it. And if their culture was being destroyed then they were colluding in the process, perhaps in the hope of advantage, that they might partake in privilege, economic or social.

There was no surrender in Tutuola's work, only the attempt to render as precisely as possible the stories from within his own culture, narrated by characters from the same culture in the oral form for the page, using both transcriptions of oral and literary techniques. This is the way out from the 'colonizer's yoke'. And when I first read the old Nigerian's stories I took it for granted, naively, that critics and academics were looking at his work in that context, doing close textual readings, comparative readings, looking at the literary and oral traditions in Nigeria and West Africa, and so on. I took it for granted because, even more naively, I had assumed they were doing that with my own.

In 1983 a collection of my stories was published. My publisher referred me to a literary magazine wherein it was reviewed. And on the same page, lo and behold, was a review of one of Tutuola's novels. It was a pleasure seeing my name alongside his. I also supposed that the shared location might offer an insight for some readers, perhaps a context for future critics and reviewers. What is it these two writers appear to share, one from Scotland and one from Nigeria? What is it that marks them out from the other writers of prose fiction under review? What do they share? What do they not share?

I was right to recognise that a context existed that brought reviews of our work together on the same page otherwise we wouldn't have been reviewed together. But what was the context? Perhaps our 'inability' to use English properly? Exactly one year later my first novel was published – The Busconductor

Hines – and denigrated by the Chairperson of the 1984 Booker Prize panel on the grounds that it was not written in English, that it contained "ugly words", that it referred to "drink, sex and violence." Even worse, remarked the Chairperson, it was "written entirely in what appeared to be Glaswegian." No critic or reviewer referred to the use of techniques normally associated with orature. It never occurred to any one of them that I might have been working in non-literary forms intentionally, rather than through ignorance.

It was assumed by most that I crept around Glasgow with recording devices at the ready, recording fearsome drunken illiterates of the Glaswegian male populace. Then I rushed home to transcribe the finished recording precisely as it sounds, and later presented this transcription to a publisher. One reviewer bestowed upon me his idea of a great compliment: "[Kelman] is an intuitive artist," said he.

I was reminded of black musicians praised for their natural rhythms while white musicians are praised for their technical expertise. A few years later I was teaching a Creative Writing course in the USA. I asked a group of European-American students to explain to me the context that allows a cartoon character in the television programme, The Simpsons – a six or seven year old European-American girl – not only to play tenor saxophone to a sophisticated level but to play it in such an acutely sensitive manner that other cartoon characters – adult African-American musicians – marvel and corroborate that de gal-chile sho nuff done got it. What done she got? Natural rhythm. All God's black jazz musicians done got that and no mistake. Whereas Benny Goodman can play Mozart's Clarinet Concerto.

A few students defended The Simpsons on the grounds that it sold all over the world so it could not be too bad. What could not be too bad? Its racism. Can we distinguish between "not too bad racism" and "racism?" Other students defended the programme on the grounds that it "gets condemned for this already."

Surely that means the programme deserves to be looked at critically? No sir, it means your personal criticism lacks originality and if you continue to criticise it along the same grounds then it is you who has a problem; some sort of chip on your shoulder. Or perhaps you are running with the majority. If a thing gets criticised once for something then it should not be criticised twice, not for the same matter. I see: so the voicing of one criticism is itself a form of punishment? The fact that the programme is condemned as racist is not grounds for critical analysis, those responsible are being punished by the condemnation, is that it? And now it is up to them, they can apologise, or not.

Other students thought "some people" have exaggerated sensitivity. If it happened to other people they might find it amusing, at least some of it. Far better that the victims of racism had a more developed sense of humour and could laugh it off. They should join with the perpetrator and take part in the ridicule of themselves.

The students thought I was overly sensitive to the 'race-question' and wondered why I should call them European-Americans when they were just Americans. I said, Well I just thought if I was to call black Americans African-Americans then I should refer to white Americans as European-Americans; and Chinese-Americans or Vietnamese-Americans, as South East Asian-Americans, and Japanese or East Russians . . .

Is there a protocol? What is the protocol?

That was the problem. I did not know the protocol. There must have been a protocol for this. This what? Infrastructural racism? Infrastructural elitism?

It is not surprising that kinship may exist between writers and further when they engage in related formal struggles. But it is surprising that this particular critical context should still remain unfathomable to what appears the majority of departments of English across the world. In fact, if one is to award these departments the benefit of the doubt, all one can say is that they have failed abysmally to do their job. I suppose this inability to acknowledge the substance of the non-assimilationist or anti-imperial voice might become a crucial part of that job.

Those who uphold the Imperial Voice of Standard English literary form sustain its prejudicial and degenerate route, unwilling to tolerate a literature that takes as given that merit may be defined by criteria other than its own.

But, ironically, T. S. Eliot was editor at Faber & Faber when they first published Tutuola. Why 'ironically'? Well, one assumes that the school of Eliot holds to be true all of that which renders the work of Tutuola less than masterly.

This partly explains why I asked to see his manuscripts when I visited the Harry Ransom Centre in Austin, Texas back in 1995. The librarian-archivist who showed us around was great. The person with me was Professor Mia Carter, a friend of mine. We spoke about old Tutuola for a few minutes. I was thinking mainly of his long fight on behalf of his culture and traditions, use of rhythms and syntax, orature and literature, transcribing the oral. I wanted to see if any heavy editorial had been practised by Eliot. Yes and I wanted to see everything but there was insufficient time: it had to be a glimpse. One exercise book is all I saw, and it looked like a late revision rather than a proper working manuscript. Of course I may be wrong.

Tutuola breathed life into the deadening voice of the colonizer; the life derives from the rhythms and speech patterns of the language(s) indigenous to his people and culture. The contemporary tradition of which he is at the heart, in direct opposition to assimilation, also reaches beyond Nigeria and Africa. It is a tradition that has endured the horrors of imperialism and at the depth of that pit has clung on at an existential level, and moved from there. His achievement was masterful for he succeeded in what for many is a contradiction in terms, he remained a tradition-bearer in a language that by all accounts can have been little other than alien.

No doubt what were then the 'Third World Studies' sections of departments of English everywhere were encouraging the study of irony and Nigerian literature, given the remarkable phenomenon that one of the most dangerous countries in the world in which to be a writer has one of its more vibrant literatures. Alongside Tutuola stand other Nigerian writers of the calibre of Chinua Achebe, Wole Soyinka, Chinweizu Ibekwe, Ben Okri, John Pepper Clark and Ken Saro-Wiwa who was murdered by due process of his government a couple of years back; at the time of writing Wole Soyinka was under sentence of death.

Agnes shrugged and got on with it

I met Agnes Owens at a writers group in the Vale of Leven more than forty-five years ago. My mother and my grandfather were both born there, in the village of Alexandria. Agnes lived in a housing scheme near Balloch. I also knew this housing scheme from my time as a nineteen year-old busconductor working for the Scottish Midland Transport company, based in the Old Kilpatrick garage. It was a tough place to work, and where Agnes stayed was a tough place to live. But there were other aspects to her place; one was the proximity of the River Leven where my grandpa developed his ability to handle a pair of oars, and another was Loch Lomond itself, whose shores lay within walking distance.

And Agnes and her family made use of that when her children were young. In those days it was possible to walk through trees to the grass by the water's edge, to build a fire and fry a panful of sausages, without being arrested for some damn thing, trespass or using a frying pan without a licence. The poet Liz Lochhead tutored the first term of the writers group and me the second. Alasdair Gray did a stint too. I returned for another year. Maybe I did another one after that. I was struggling to make a living. Who wasn't?

As can happen in community writers groups a schoolteacher dominated proceedings; not always a male but in this one it was. Agnes shrugged and got on with it. Her stories were so different. The others in the group didn't know what to make of them. This included the dominant schoolteacher. The rug was pulled from under him by the visiting tutors; Liz, Alasdair and myself; we knew what she was doing, she was writing great stories. Already she was working from her own experience in a way that required her to break the rules. Her stories were barely recognised as "real" stories by the other members. I don't think she was patronised but it ran close to that. Her need to break the rules was interpreted as ignorance of the rules. But she wore them down.

Agnes' work forced people to question the nature of value, literary and societal; not simply the values themselves but how these values come about in the first place. It is not that 'the rules of the English language' are right or wrong, but why are they there and what purpose do they serve? The truth of the world created by Agnes was revealed in her work, and starkly present for those who dared read it. Many people did. Many writers did. She enjoyed the company of other writers and enjoyed this aspect of Glasgow. There weren't so many in the Balloch area and she missed that conversation. Over the years she was attached to a few writers groups locally. She was treated with respect, with affection, and enormous pride.

What I Do

I know she was writing as a young person. She told me. In that she reminded me of Jeff Torrington whose experience as a writer was similar. People thought they began in middle age. It is not true. The circumstances forced them to give their best time and energy to earning a wage. When Agnes joined that Vale of Leven writers group in the mid-1970s she was continuing something she had begun years before. This is reminiscent also of the American writer Tillie Olsen who wrote three quarters of a novel at the age of nineteen then went off, had a large family and lived a life of ordinary domestic drudgery into her forties. One day rooting about in her attic she found the unfinished story, and resumed her work. Later she wrote a magnificent work of non-fiction, Silences, in which she explores the effects of economic slavery and domestic drudgery on creativity and on the lives of various writers, almost all of whom were women. She and Agnes would have enjoyed one another's company.

Agnes' life was quite extraordinary, attempting to make ends meet as a working-class mother of seven children, working at various jobs throughout her adult life to ensure the family's survival. She had endured the death of her first husband at the age of forty-three then the murder of her youngest son Patrick, only nineteen years old. This was an horrific event only compounded by the legal system's failure to deal adequately with the crime. More recently was the death of her daughter Irene, a terrible blow to Agnes and her family.

The characters she created confront the day-to-day at a level of nightmare that horrifies many. Society denies the truth and turns from it. People are no longer useful. The concept 'citizen' is outdated. Nowadays we have stakeholders, shareholders, and a burgeoning 'service industry'. The rich and powerful require service, and servants provide it. Shareholders have a right to vote. Unfortunately not everyone holds a share and vast monopolies of shares may be held by a tiny few individuals who can make them count in whatever way they choose. It is their right to pursue their own individual interest to the last breath in their body. This system is designed such that vast inequalities of wealth are created. It is government's duty to provide the conditions that will allow extreme wealth to be hoarded safely, and where possible increased. As part of the process state institutions inflict upon the poor and working-class an ethical and cultural value system that helps smash them further into the ground. The moral life becomes 'the good life', a confused jumble of religious obligation, etiquette and keeping up with the Joneses. There is no justice. No common good. Only 'grab' what ye can while ye can.

Agnes understood her community and from within it made the greatest art. She knew shopfloor politics and had been a shop steward. She would have been fearless, but pragmatic too I reckon. She had been a member of the Labour Party since a young woman and could not conceive of a viable socialist alternative. We did the occasional reading together and had a few arguments over the years. She was not negative towards the Communist Party but my kind of antiparliamentarian politics merely exasperated her.

In her stories children, men and women struggle to survive. Society is revealed. Its custodians employ battalions of highly-educated servants, assisted by skilled security operatives, to perpetuate the swindle through propaganda, mystification and disinformation. Institutional bullying and harassment aid the process. There may well be a 'moral imperative' but whether or not individuals live by this is 'their right'. Nobody is forced to live morally, especially the rich and powerful. In societies of this nature, writers and artists who concentrate on universal aspects of humanity are feted and rewarded: those whose work engage with reality are marginalized. Empathy becomes the key. Attention is focused on the inviolable humanity of 'our' royalty, the inherent value of 'our' aristocracy, the disciplined integrity of 'our' upper classes; the lives and loves of 'our' multi-millionaire sports stars and movie stars; the cool enigma of 'our' billionaire financiers.

What is it that the highest of the high will share with the lowest of the low? Search it out and write about it. Everybody likes a swim and a nice glass of wine; everybody has 'a relation-ship'; everybody wants sex, is scared of ghosts and aliens, suspicious of strangers, loves a superhero; needs a doctor when ill or calls a cop whenever they stumble upon a person murdered by a crazed psychopath.

This is reflected in the literary worlds of fantasy that abound. The stuff that ignores reality fills the shelves of bookshops; in the world of television and movies fantasy fills the screen. For 85 or 90 percent of the world it is all fantasy anyway, not just the other-worldly beings and the superheroes who respect God and the Constitution but the cool detective dudes, heroic doctors, good-natured nurses, sexy lawyers and down-to-earth judges.

Agnes had no option but to work, and work she did in factories and cleaning the homes of wealthy people and she went on doing it even as a published writer. Without Alasdair Gray's help and encouragement she might never have written these last stories, as she herself mentioned:

> Alasdair said, why don't you write more short stories. I showed one to him and he went squeaky with delight, like he does. So, I thought, maybe I'm not finished. Maybe I'll show you some more.

It is marvellous that she did and the perseverance of Alasdair must be appreciated. He stuck to the task and when it comes to cracking tough nuts, well, who was more stubborn than Agnes?

I think people were in awe of her. This includes many writers. No wonder. When Agnes was at her strongest there was none stronger. Sometimes tears are our only response. Few writers produce this effect. The stories closest to me are those where women are central. I see the strength Agnes had as a female strength. It is there in the characters who inhabit her fictions. It is not that these women are survivors, and many do not survive, but they engage in a struggle which is virtually insurmountable.

They fight tooth and claw towards an end. This 'end' is taken for granted by a society that expects them to do likewise and punishes them ruthlessly when they don't. This 'end' is the survival, health and well-being of their children and young people.

Society denies its culpability and conceals reality. The pretence is maintained not only by its custodians but by those who fail to engage in the struggle. In much of Agnes Owens' fiction the menfolk not only capitulate they do not support their female partners, and some never forgive them for fighting on. That very fight illustrates their own shortcomings; perhaps also their cowardice. It brings to mind a sentence from the last story in Agnes' The Complete Short Stories collection:

> We both kicked and struggled and I believe I would've got the better of her, if a strange man hadn't come in, got hold of us, and pushed us into a van as though we were dogs being taken to the dog pound.

The first-person narrator is a young girl, alongside her wee brother. Thematic elements include the absence of responsible parents and the fight to survive at all costs; the female as 'lead' protagonist in a mixed gender relationship; and a mysterious all-powerful male figure who either has the backing and bless-ing of society, or is able to act as though that is the case. The story is entitled *The Dysfunctional Family*, written by Agnes in her eighties. It echoes *The Lighthouse*, a wonderful story she wrote years earlier.

Polygon Books published her collected stories in 2008. To celebrate the publication she did a few reading events and I was with her at the book festivals in Edinburgh and Milngavie, the town of her girlhood. There was a tremendous warmth towards her from both audiences. Even Agnes had to see that. I said it to her: They just love ye. She gave me that beautiful smile, the one that makes me greet now. Her realization of the truth of what I was saying, quickly undercut by that laconic grin, Well Jim . . . and whatever she said then, I cannot recollect. But she knew it, she knew that that love was there towards her.

Several weeks before she died Alasdair and I visited her and Pat, her husband. She was not getting around easily. There were the physical indignities too but she put up with them in that ironic manner she had and which I had come to know since that Vale of Leven writers group of the late 1970s. In the thirty-five years I knew her she lacked the freedom to explore her art with consistency of practice. Those in a position to support her through the public purse failed to act. She wasn't this and she wasn't that and never seemed 'to qualify'. Yet against the odds she created an art that will endure. Her best stories are great stories. Shout it from the rooftops: Agnes Owens was a great writer, and she was also a great woman, a strong fighting woman.

The writer John Mulligan

John was the eldest of ten children and seventeen years-old when his family emigrated to the USA from Kirkintilloch in Scotland. They landed in Indianapolis in 1968 during the heat of the Vietnam War. Conscription was then in effect and young men and women such as John Mulligan had no choice in the matter. Within weeks he was called up and entered the Air Force.

The experience was traumatic and might have destroyed his life entirely. He later married and had a daughter and two sons but the effects of the war lived on for him. He suffered what became identified as post-traumatic stress disorder. His life fell apart, his marriage broke up and he finished on the street, fighting alcohol and drug addiction, along with tens of thousands of other Vietnam veterans who traversed the country, pushing their belongings about in shopping carts.

I met him in the mid-1990s when he was working on his novel Shopping Cart Soldiers, based on his time in Vietnam. This was in San Francisco where also I saw the guy on the street who became an important figure in my novel You have to be Careful in the Land of the Free. He was the ghostly, mythical character pushing the shopping cart with his belongings. God knows what belongings he had inside the cart but the only visible clothing on his back was one overcoat. There were not enough buttons to close it. He had nothing else, no shoes, no trousers; nothing. He had to keep pushing with one hand and hold the overcoat closed with his other. What had happened? A war had happened. It was degrading to witness. He was not degraded, we were. He was a man and that was his condition, and passing along, head down and pushing, pushing, nowhere to go and nothing ahead but horrors. This was broad daylight, late morning or early afternoon. People did not see him. Anyway, they appeared not to.

This was on the famous Haight Street. John's partner lived closeby on Ashbury Street and she had kindly allowed myself and two friends to stay there for a couple of nights. I was on my own walking at the time I saw the guy with the shopping cart. If I had been with John something would have happened. I have no doubt about that. The guy with the cart would not have been avoided. I don't know what might have happened had John been there, but something, definitely.

On one occasion I was with him he stopped to have a word with guys living on the street and I heard one call him by his second name, Mulligan, as he was known also in his favoured local café. He knew these men as if one himself, and he was, now and again. John was domiciled in San Francisco and for sustained periods fought his way off the streets and out of that situation which was not a hopeless one entirely, otherwise he could not have contrived to escape it. But it was close to hopeless; too close for comfort and too close for most people. That world would suck you back, the unbearable injustice of it for tens of thousands of Vietnam veterans, denied their rightful support from the US State, becoming an embarrassment to American society. San Francisco is in some ways a beautiful city, at least to visit, but you are never far from the other side of society and it is difficult to not see the huge numbers of people attempting to survive on the streets.

John not only involved himself in the struggle for justice waged by these Vietnam veterans he took a leading role in it and this role intensified when word broke on his novel. At an earlier period he had enrolled in a creative writing group at the University of California, Berkeley, organised for the veterans by a very fine writer, Maxine Hong Kingston, who strongly encouraged him.

Before Shopping Cart Soldiers was published he had a small apartment in North Bay, a stone's throw from Café Trieste and just round the corner from the City Lights Bookshop. They have photographs of former writer-customers of whom there have been many. I hope they have one of John Mulligan. This café was his favourite hang-out. This is a good part of San Francisco, perhaps more for adults than children. You can walk down to the wharfs and dockside, step aboard the old Balclutha clipper, built by Charlie Connell, a carpenter to trade on the River Clyde. Later he owned a shipyard at Scotstoun West.

Balclutha translates as "town on the Clyde": Glasgow, although its maiden voyage sailed from Swansea. I wish I had known the story of the Balclutha when John was alive. He would have enjoyed the information. The Balclutha was a nice old boat and used to ply the waters from San Francisco to Alaska: they renamed it the Spirit of Alaska during that period; you can go on board and see the history of it all. There are always people on board, schoolkids, helpers and tourists. Things Scottish did interest him. Not only the Glasgow connection although that would have appealed to him.

But no doubt he knew it all already, and would have given me one of these vaguely surprised looks. Maybe it was the time he spent on the streets. If somebody said something daft he was never quite sure what the formalities were, should he tell me or not. He also assumed I was loaded and scoffed when I told him the reality. He really did think I was kidding. A US publisher had just produced a selection of my stories entitled Busted Scotch, so that plus the Booker Prize was enough for John. It equated to dough, it had to. He refused to believe I was still scraping by. When he finally accepted the bad news he said he was going to move into the movie business. He was undaunted, even exhilarated. The idea of all the work he still had to do *was* exhilarating. I wondered if this was how people felt coming out of prison. The potential, the anticipation. He was so excited by the future, all the ideas and wild ventures; all these plans for short stories and essays and plays and screenplays and a new novel and oh fuck man the world was just so marvellously big . . . when one is not borne under by the trials and the tribulations.

There was only one time I was with John that he did go back on the booze. And that was back in Scotland, he had made a trip home. We went to the Clutha Bar in Glasgow where we met a couple of other writers and sank a few pints of Guinness. The English edition of Shopping Cart Soldiers had by this time appeared and he came to Britain to help with the publicity, and steal some time in Scotland. He really enjoyed it. This was his first visit home for many many years. He stayed over with me and Marie for a couple of nights. I drove him out to Kirkin-tilloch to meet up with cousins, nephews and nieces, most of whom he had never seen. We were driving along the road into a side scheme when he thought he recognised a niece walking along the street. We stopped the car and he walked to her.

And he was right; she was his niece. The girl turned and saw him and she went right to him, a huge huge cuddle. Then he returned to the car for his suitcase. We shook hands and so on, and that was the last time I ever saw him.

John was such an impressive man, and that particular patience he had, I recognized that too. I see this form of patience quite rarely, but it is there in men who are used to violence, who deal with it as and where necessary, when matters reach a certain stage. What is the stage? How far will that patience stretch? You are never quite sure and better not finding out.

We did not keep in touch. I heard only rare snippets of news from his friend Alan Black, manager of San Francisco's

Edinburgh Castle Pub. It was through Alan Black's support that John was brought into the acquaintance of visiting Scottish writers. And Alan had been instrumental in bringing a few Scottish writers to perform at this pub. In the upstairs space he made it a wee theatre, and staged Liz Lochhead's Mary Queen of Scots Got Her Head Chopped Off. John read with myself, Alan Warner, Irvine Welsh, Kevin Williamson and Brendan McLaughlin. He visited Tillie Olsen in the company of Maxine Hong Kingston. John not only thought Robert Louis Stevenson was the greatest Scottish writer of all time, he assumed this was a simple fact of life and was astonished that not everyone agreed – including me, although I do like and respect his work. It was on safer ground with Kris Kristofferson for whom we shared respect and appreciation.

R.L.S. also spent time in California and much of this in the Bay area. There is a plaque to him on a house in San Francisco which I saw one morning by accident, when I was going over the hill for a very early morning coffee. R.L.S. also stayed for a time north of San Francisco then for a period farther south, in Monterey where a small museum – the Stevenson House – is devoted to him. It was closed the day me and my wife Marie showed up.

In Scotland the Anglophile bias and bureaucracy are such that the Scottish public hardly know the names of their own artists, never mind accord them memorials. This would have surprised John. He had a romantic view of Scotland and assumed it was a great wee country, full of bravehearts moving ever forward to independence. It may well move to independence, but it will never be a great wee country for as long as it ignores its own artists.

One time in the late 1990s I was back in San Francisco and with Brendan McLaughlin we went along to Café Trieste to see if John was around, but he was not, and had not been seen for a while. We heard he had gone back on the streets following publication of his novel. And he had, but then once more that tremendous fighting spirit, the indefatigable Mulligan clawed himself back together.

Shopping Cart Soldiers is a beautiful and original piece of work. Following its publication, as I said earlier, John gave much of his time and energy to the plight endured by veterans, particularly of the Vietnam War, victims of post-traumatic stress disorder. He knew of it intimately through direct personal experience. I was not with him often enough to know a great deal of his involvement but he did mention it on occasion. In fact, he had gone on to become

one of the most respected voices in the [US] on the travails of troubled veterans. Even after falling into homelessness again after his novel came out, he steeled himself back to stability . . . to pen parts of four more novels, short stories and a book giving advice to other vets on post-traumatic stress disorder – and he was about to get married. That all ended at 9:51 p.m. on Oct. 12 [2005], when the 55-year-old author was crossing a busy street near his Mountain View home, pizza in hand for himself and his fiancée. He was wearing dark clothes on a dark night. A car hit him, and he died instantly.[1]

The worst imaginable. How that would have been for his family. It is beyond anything. I did not hear the circumstances until later when I was living and working at the local university, not far from Mountain View which is a suburb of San José, a couple of hours drive from Stevenson House, Monterey.

What a life, what a loss. His name is unknown in Scotland and is likely to remain so but not in California; in particular San Francisco which came to be his city and he belongs to that great pantheon of writers we associate with it.

"Rocking the Boat"[1]

Leslie Forster was born in 1919 and died in 2016, the last living member of the group of Glasgow comrades who left the Communist Party of Great Britain in the early 1950s. These included Harry McShane, Hugh Savage and, later, Ned Donaldson and Matt McGinn among others. Their activism only increased outwith the yoke of the CPGB.

Leslie's father and grandfather were from Leith originally. They came to Glasgow before the 1st World War, opening a blacksmith's shop at the corner of Bilsland Drive and Maryhill Road, a two-storey tenement building. Leslie and his big brother Archie were born there. "The kitchen window looked down on the blacksmith's shop." Their blacksmith grandpa was over six feet tall and "a believer in physical force." He once caught a burglar in his home, lifted him to the window and dropped him out. They held the contract for shoeing horses at the military barracks by the Wyndford, adjacent to the old Maryhill railway station. They also shoed the horses for the annual circus and zoo that toured into the Kelvin Hall.

Leslie's mother was a Munro from Brora. This coastal region in Sutherland is where thousands ended up waiting to be shipped to Canada, cleared off the land by the Duke and Duchess of Sutherland, the worst of landowner aristocracy. Some stayed and tried scratching a living off the shore and the sea. Instead of doing that Leslie's grandfather, a stonemason, emigrated to Glasgow; he too found work at the military barracks.

Les and his brother attended Garrioch Primary then Allan Glen's School. Archie was seven years older. Les always spoke well of him. Not only did he go to Glasgow University he was a hustler at snooker. He learned the game at Johnnie May's billiard saloon which was less than a hundred yards along Maryhill Road, in that one-storey building next to the garage.

Unlike his brother, Les had little time for school, nor its "history books . . . 'Gung Ho' propaganda tracts" he called them, "heavily laced with Rule Britannia. Our tiny feet marching to the strains of Onward Christian Soldiers." He went his own way, and left school early.

Sometimes I feel like throwing up when I hear pundits talking about the dignity of labour. One Monday morning I sold my dignity to a company called the Saracen Foundry, by the time Friday came round I asked for it back . . . I began to study the moulders' physique . . . a complexion of ashen grey, sunken cheeks, backs permanently bent, old before their time . . . sparks flying all over the place, odd bits of burning ingot dropped onto the floor. I asked the gaffer for my cards – and got them.

Later he entered the building trade as a plasterer's labourer, reading voraciously, keeping his eyes and ears open. His family moved to Milngavie but his heart was in Maryhill. He was eighteen when his dad died. He and his mother flitted back to Glasgow, to a tenement flat in Garnethill. She was politicised and attended political meetings, and was a friend of Johnny Muir of the Clyde Workers Committee. When Leslie got involved politically she encouraged him.

He joined the Communist Party and in his early twenties became Secretary of the City Branch. This was where he met James 'Jimmy' McLaren of the same age-group and already holding office. McLaren was from Binnie Place at Brigton Cross; not only treasurer to the City Communist Party Committee, he was also Secretary of his local branch. A year later he and Les Forster met with another young fellow, Hugh Savage.

The three remained close pals as well as close comrades until McLaren died tragically of tuberculosis at the age of twenty-eight. He had been an all-round activist: organiser, motivator, orator, campaigner, as well as theoretician and educator. When he died his books were shared between the other two, and many of those were passed on to myself. He had a tremendous range as a reader: politics, philosophy, science, mathematics. Les and Hugh cherished scraps of his lecture notes and commentaries. His family had a reputation around Brigton, not for the finer activities in life, and Les would smile: Jimmy was the white-sheep of the family. They always spoke of him with affection but there was an additional factor that I gathered, the sense that Jimmy was the one who would leave his mark.

But all three did that. In preparation for his own death, McLaren asked that Bill Laughlan lead the service at his funeral and wrote of him that "he was glad to have worked under such a capable fellow." The other official whom McLaren mentions in a positive light was Sam Aaronovitch. Les Forster had a different opinion, based on later experiences: "when myself and others were having doubts about party policy, Aaronovitch remained an out and out diehard. Even when I left the CP he was still an unrepentant Stalinist."

Like many young Glasgow communists McLaren, Forster and Savage were taught to be wary of Harry McShane. Among the stalwarts McShane had a fearsome reputation for 'awkward individualism.' He said what he thought and acted accordingly, and it didn't sit well with Party chiefs. Not so for the younger comrades who were avid readers, avid thinkers, eager for theory and activists to the core. The ability to think for yourself went down just fine with them.

In Glasgow the lack of housing for working-class people has been a central issue for generations. The fight was carried by Harry McShane among others and his impact on the younger generation was keenly felt.

The Grand Hotel at Charing Cross was used as a club by the American Army during the War. Later it stood empty – a must for potential squatters. So Harry McShane, Bill

McCulloch, Bob Saunders and myself broke in through a side door taking in tow a fair number of families. Crowds gathered, the Police arrived, sirens blazing. Several Party Leaders stood there without lifting a hand to help. When the Assistant Chief Constable saw Harry McShane come out the front door he said, I might have known . . .

Leslie by then was a Shop Steward in the building trade and he became a leader of the Merrylee Housing struggle of 1951, along with another young comrade, a bricklayer by the name of Ned Donaldson "who organised massive protests on building trade issues." The CPGB hierarchy thought him "too prone to acting independently . . . without the 'firm guidance of the Party.'"[2] The Tory council wanted to sell off 622 council houses at a time when 100,000 people were on the council waiting list in Glasgow.

In those days workers did not get pestered by the absurd rigmarole of postal ballots. Decisions were made at the point of production. After discussion and debate a vote was taken. Those in favour one side . . . those against the other. The strike lasted ten days. Guy Aldred's Strickland Press printed 30,000 leaflets for the strike and when told the committee were skint Guy said forget it, it's a worthwhile cause.

The Tories lost that one but in the aftermath Les was sacked. He and Ned were blacklisted. This was the end of the building trade for Les; he joined British Rail and stayed there until his retiral. But he remained politically committed, and intellectually active, and with a few friends and comrades developed the space for a more radical approach.[3]

In 1953 he, Hugh Savage and Bill McCulloch resigned from the Communist Party alongside Harry McShane and took to 'spreading the message'; chalking pavements, publishing The New Commune and the Socialist Revolt, and generally being a left-wing thorn in the side of the CPGB.

> Lenin's Last Will and Testament had been suppressed by the Soviet Communist Party. The British Party made sure it never saw the time of day. In the will, Lenin, after making a number of serious criticisms said that Stalin was dangerous and unfit to don the mantle of Leader. We procured the text and published.

One night Les, Hugh, Harry McShane and Matt McGinn[4] were up in Bill McCulloch's house[5] planning stuff. A chap at the door. Gerry Healy of the Workers Revolutionary Party (WRP) was up from London on a recruiting mission, expressly to check out the radical dissidents. He was wasting his time. They had had enough of vanguards. "Our aim was to go it alone, no pretensions or ambitions . . . we thought there was a great need for Socialist Propaganda, and nothing more than that . . . We took to the soap box holding regular open air meetings at the corner of Drury Street. Controversy was encouraged, questions never fudged." At one such meeting in bleak November two hundred people turned up on the anniversary of John

Maclean's death. But later "We ran out of cash [and] our paper, Socialist Revolt, was put to sleep. Alas only three of us soldiered on, Hugh Savage, Harry McShane and myself – we still remained revolutionary 'socialists.'"

Leslie continued in British Rail, always working on his own research and writing projects. He contributed to the Glasgow Labour History Project; wrote on the 1911 Clydebank Singer Strike[6] and the crucial role of women there, the old Socialist Labour Party (SLP) and the Wobblies too, the Industrial Workers of the World. He wrote a history of the National Union of Railwaymen and did the Introduction for McShane's Three Days That Shook Edinburgh.[7] He and Hugh Savage published a life of the forgotten nineteenth century Marxist, Willie Nairn,[8] who influenced a generation of working-class activists, including John Maclean, Arthur McManus, Willie Paul, Neil Maclean and Tom Bell.

He was a font of local knowledge, from cinemas and back-street singers to the political agitations. George Millar stabbed to death by a blackleg in 1834 during the printers' strike at Dawsholm, buried at the old cemetery at the corner of Duart Street and Maryhill Road. Keir Hardie's ashes? Here at the Western Necropolis. A memorial stone to Donald Macrae, the Alness martyr? Right here, where they buried him. What about the Chartist leader Arthur O'Neil leading off the Maryhill contingent from Gilshochill, led by an Orange flute band, probably from the same Lodge that glares back at ye to this day, when ye look up the hill at Sandbank Street.

Les laughed at that but was touchy on certain subjects. One learned to tread cautiously. But he was always interested in people. His first questions were on your family and his interest was genuine.

He was a passionate man. Politics, radical history, football and Maryhill were his primary subjects – unless he was talking about his wife. She died in 2005. Her name was Grace and they did everything together. Without her he was cast adrift. In those days I was watching the local football team, Maryhill Juniors. They play home games at Lochburn Park which is less than a quarter of an hour's walk from where I stay. I invited Les along and he was keen to come. Even more than football he loved Maryhill, so Maryhill Juniors gave him the best of both. It was getting out to watch the 'Hill that helped him through the worst period of his life, the dark time following Gracie's death.

He was not the easiest of companions. People who didn't know him thought he was and certainly he was companionable; he always engaged with folk and wanted to hear what they had to say. The difficulty was if somebody came out with nonsense he was liable to confront them. And in ordinary pub conversations people are apt to come out with nonsense, especially on matters of a political bent, and it pays to remember that in Glasgow religion is a subset of politics. (Leslie, a frail old guy of 90, angrily confronting the pub bully, Who do you think ye're talking to? And the pub goes quiet, and the pub bully gets a riddy and steals off to the toilet.)

In the 1980s Leslie, Hugh Savage and Ned Donaldson came out of 'political retirement' and were in at the early stages of Workers City. Alongside Janette McGinn, Freddie and Isobel Anderson, Farquhar McLay and other friends and comrades, they went to war with Glasgow City Council, and political corruption in general. Les was back writing again. He wrote a couple of pieces for that 'scurrilous rag' of fond memory, the 'Keelie! He also found time to write his autobiography and left many unpublished articles.

At the end he was talking football, politics, music, and memories, and reading Kropotkin's The Conquest of Bread, then aged ninety-six.

He had been in hospital since August; in a Maryhill nursing home since early December, a stone's throw from his family's blacksmith shop down Bilsland Drive. He was making the best of a bad lot. A few days earlier he had been transferred to the Royal Infirmary, with the breathing mask back on his mouth, tubes poking out everywhere. He was skin and bone and it was purgatory. He was completely fed up with it all. This and the knowledge that once recovered it was back to the nursing home. He was never going home. No, that wasn't a life.

His friends and comrades spoke about 'contributions'. The biggest compliment you could pay a comrade, "what a contribution!" Well that was Leslie Forster, to the Labour movement and the Socialist movement, a lifetime's commitment, what a contribution.

Oh sorry, wrong room

A number of western heroes have emerged from Lubbock, Texas. I see Joe Slate as one. He embodied that better side of the State, too often missing in the stereotype. While he took pleasure in local matters cultural and historical, it was from an utterly un-parochial and cosmopolitan perspective. He was never afraid of being an intellectual or being seen to love art. He had a specialist's knowledge not only of James Joyce and William Carlos Williams but the Cisco Kid and Pancho, and a majority of the movie novelizations ever written. The bulk of the latter were unreadable, according to Joe, although he had read them all. And been obliged to, I would say, otherwise on whose authority could he have made the judgment!

In 1998, accompanied by my wife Marie, I came to teach at UT Austin for a couple of years, and we returned on occasion during the following years. Our regard for Texas was fixed in place by those who befriended us in those early days. Among them Joe Slate and his wife Patricia were to the fore.

Joe taught at UT for forty-five years. Patricia was part-owner, founder and full-time operator of the famous old Sweetish Hill Bakery.[1]

Joe did not drive; highly unusual in Texas. Most mornings he walked to his campus office and generally travelled home by bus. I did not see him moving too often. He seemed to flit about the place. Either he was there or not. I never met anyone else who walked and took buses. He had no career ambitions I ever noticed, other than improving his capacity to teach and to teach properly. He was capable of the most withering of looks. No student would have enjoyed being at the wrong end of that. Joe hated racism, elitism, sexism. He hated injustice. He did get irritated by stuff, especially humbug and the academic world has become suffocated by that. Maybe this is why Joe preferred flitting in and out of campus, maintaining close links only with students and certain colleagues. It was no coincidence that he remained friends with the legendary James Sledd.[2] It was through Joe, my wife and myself came to know Jim Sledd and his wife Joan and became friends for the last years of Jim's life.

But that too had an aspect to it that I had forgotten about; before I came to UT Austin I was in correspondence with Noam Chomsky and he advised me there was someone in the Austin area that I should meet if I got the chance: Jim Sledd.[3] Then about a week before I left Glasgow for Texas I received a direct telephone call from Sean Connery in Los Angeles who bemoaned the idea that I was having to leave Scotland to take a job. He gave me the name of one person he thought I would enjoy meeting up with: the movie screenwriter Bill Broyles. The interesting point here is that I met both Jim Sledd and Bill Broyles through Joe Slate, purely in the natural course of events; at one time or another both attended the 'potluck' nights organised by Patricia with Joe's assistance.

Pals of mine came along for the trip from Glasgow, Scotland. They came on a few occasions and were very appreciative of Joe and Patricia. One abiding memory was a certain fundraising quiz night at a West 6th Street Bar round about 2005, the year after Joe's retirement. This was on behalf of Rude Mechanicals Music Theatre company. One of the questions was: how many Scotsmen were killed at the Alamo? One of the guys from the Scottish table shouted: All of them!

Maybe the quickest wit in the room but the Scottish team failed to win the competition. Joe's team did, he sat at a table with a few of his former students; they won the quiz 'out the park'. I never discovered who had organized the questions.

On one jaunt into the Hill Country Marie and I were with Joe and Patricia. It was following a flood and while wandering the banks of the Guadalupe River we found a wee place with a stack of flint workings, where arrow-heads had been manufactured. Other long weekends we enjoyed down in Nuevo Laredo. Another trip brought us to the annual Cajun-Zydeco Festival in Lafayette, Louisiana. If we hadn't gone there at the invitation of Joe and Patricia then I would never have written the novel Dirt Road. During the weekend we had a night at the Evangeline horse racing track.

What I Do

Boozoo Chavis lived in these parts. I came across his music in 1971 from a superb double-album entitled Nothing but the Blues. I bought it in Kelvinbridge, Glasgow out of an old-style quality newsagent which sold books and music as well as newspapers, journals and magazines. A marvellous introduction to the blues. Among all the great tracks there was one that sounded that bit different – to me anyway. This had been recorded in 1954 someplace around Lake Charles, Louisiana. The song was *Forty Days*, by Boozoo Chavis and his Orchestra; and the musical genre was listed as 'zodico'. I put his name in the notebook.

On one occasion Boozoo earned decent cash from his music and set up as a horse trainer at that Lafayette Evangeline racetrack. It was a strange style of horse racing where the races themselves were around one furlong in length. During our visit to the festival we managed a night at the track. I did not bet a winner, and lost out on a twenty-five to one shot. I had pointed out the name of this horse to Marie, Patricia and Joe, because it shared the name of one of my students who happened to originate from Louisiana, a young woman who wrote very promising stories. What a coincidence it was! Unfortunately I was always a scientific sort of gambler, a form student, and would never bet on anything connected to "luck". Thus, obviously, the horse won, and I hadn't a bean on it.

On the trip home from Lafayette I played Joe the wonderful Beau Jocque recording of *Cisco Kid*. Joe may have been an expert on Ceesco and Pancho, but that was a first for him.

Oh sorry, wrong room

The Cisco Kid was a friend of mine
The Cisco Kid was a friend of mine
He drink whiskey, Poncho drink the wine
He drink whiskey, Poncho drink the wine

We had many good times together. Every away trip we made was so much the better for the packed picnic hampers Patricia had towed behind the car. There were six of us one evening in Nuevo Laredo in a horse-betting bar and restaurant; our friends Susie and Jamie Valentine were along with us. I phoned home to Scotland for a quick chat with one of my daughters. She told me I had just been awarded a cash prize for a collection of my stories. I ordered a bottle of champagne discreetly and had it delivered anonymously to our table, with the compliments of an unknown benefactor. I didn't tell anyone, apart from Marie in a whispered aside. Joe had an encyclopaedic mind, but he remained flummoxed by that one.

I have a strong image of him in the old house on Highland Avenue, smoking a salmon for one of those 'pot luck' nights. I found his company relaxing. If one had nothing to say then respect the silence. No need to be talking out of politeness but fine if you did; that twinkle in his eye when he dropped some tidbit of information and blinked through the smoke for your reaction. While I replenished the red wine Joe smoked the fish. I think he did anyway. I could hardly distinguish him for the mosquitoes buzzing around his fizzog. He never seemed too bothered by their presence. Maybe they didn't feed off him. It would not have surprised me if they had left him alone. Joe was as good around other species as he was with humankind. He had an unsentimental and essential love toward animals that we associate with country people. Maybe it was reciprocated by the mosquitoes, maybe they got as much pleasure as myself from the sound and the quality of Joe's laughter.

I always thought about Joe that he could have climbed on a horse and galloped from Highland Avenue to some Higher Senate convened meeting of professors, upper strata bureaucrats and would-be statesmen, dismounted with precision and entered the meeting utterly unruffled. Obviously he would have been wearing an immaculate western suit, complete with leather boots, string tie and longhorn brooch, topped by a black Parisian beret borrowed from Thelonius Monk. Joe would have taken one look at this Higher Senate convened meeting, and muttered: Oh sorry, wrong room. [4]

Tom[1]

Tom Leonard never represented any group or party in his life. He is the embodiment of the individual: the living, breathing unique self. Spiritually, existentially. People from throughout Scotland, Ireland, England and Wales would have wanted to be here today; from different parts of the world. Many are. His life exemplified the courage and the heroism of one person, one human being. This is expressed in him, in his self and in his work – a body of work that is unsurpassable.

What are the terms we apply, the attributes of Tom Leonard? Integrity, honesty, passion; absolute commitment, absolute faith, faith in life, in the living. Was there ever a *more* spiritual man?

We had a few strong individuals in and around the city, fifty years ago. We still have. People prepared to enter the struggle, to return the fight, to carry it forward. Tom was one, at the age of twenty-one or twenty-two, he was an instant hero with his Six Glasgow Poems. And for more than fifty years he has remained a hero.

Tom never stopped. Through thick and thin, good health and bad he kept on working, helping, supporting, never afraid to nail his colours to the mast. In solidarity. He fought for what he believed. He met everything head on, everything and everyone. As far as 'flyting' goes Tom led the field, up there with old Dunbar.

Those times one thought, Tom Tom, take it easy, they aren't worth it. But for Tom everyone was worth it. He did take it on. Everyone *deserved* to be taken on. People he knew as enemies. Each one was a human being. And *deserved* to be treated as a human being. So Tom did. And he waded right in, punch for punch. What do ye mean? What do ye mean what do ye mean! Hang on a minute! Ye're no getting away with that!

And in he went, all that physical and emotional energy, intellectual passion, engaging, confronting. Tom gave it all, and we worried for him, we worried for him.

Tom loved many people. And many of those are discovered in his work: composers, musicians, visual artists; doctors and philosophers, theologians, poets, playwrights; prose-writers clunking along . . . Plus assorted members of Celtic Football Club.

Okay 1967 was important, the European Cup and all that. But 1957! What about that! Tom's amazing fitba scrapbook that he kept from boyhood! Some of you here today have seen it. Mochan, Peacock, Evans, Fernie, Wilson, Collins, McPhail – Charlie Tully! In 1957 Tom's favourite song was a calypso. I'll gie ye the first line:

> *Oh Island in the Sun,*
> *(Celtic seven, Rangers one.)*

Tom

Apologies to Harry Belafonte who wrote and sang the original; thanks for the melody.

Tom's tradition takes from anywhere and gives to anyone. The local is primary. Tom insists on this, both as starting place and as end place. The local *is* the universal. It's not going anywhere. True universalism. This is a living community, and we fight for the living community; a community of free-thinking individuals. In solidarity.

This is what makes his work so radical, so dangerous; anathema to authority. That is Tom's tradition. This is how I see it. Tom's lifework. All of it. His beautiful poetry; the drawings, posters and sketches, cartoons; songs and music, his wonderful satire, brilliant essays; and the blogs, and the journal. All of it. Leave it alone. It's one thing. That is Tom's work, his lifework. Don't touch it, don't divide it. It is one thing. It is a complete thing of the one man. Don't meddle with that.

Aonghas Macneacail, friend of Tom for fifty years, doesn't see Tom as a pioneer at all, he is the pinnacle. I see this too. One cannot reach beyond.

Tom was a master. In recent times he was back working on Places of the Mind, his book on B. V. Thomson and these preoccupations Tom held from boyhood: good and evil, innocence, guilt, right and wrong; sin *a priori*, freedom and providence; where an older philosophy meets existentialism: Augustine, Eriugena, Duns Scotus, Aquinas, Kierkegaard, Buber. More heroes. *Many* masters. That is the tradition.

Its heart is a community, an ever-expanding community. Nobody is excluded. Self-identify! Whoever ye are! We may not separate literature, art, politics, music, theology, science: teaching as demystification, tradition bearing; generation through generation.

Where truth is authorized, 'it is not necessary to think,' as somebody once said.

People cope with authorized 'truth' from various sources, sources that may be vouchsafed by society but which individuals learn not to trust, to seek clarification. Authorities aren't keen on clarity. They see it as a challenge. Heresy! Let the punishment begin: marginalization, censorship, suppression, withdrawal of resources. People learn to haud their wheesht. Others persist and take it as far as they can, they begin from the beginning: how they speak, how they think, how they breathe.

How is your breath this morning?

Tom's presence . . . Did he write that?

No, I did. Tom is that kind of writer. We work away on our own writing and become aware of his presence, his patterns of thought. He was a Christian some of the time, an atheist some of the time, an agnostic some of the time, and for much of the time antagonistic to each of those, reaching to where the negation entitles its own field, a belief-system in itself.

What do ye mean truth? Your truth is not my truth. If I say truth as we know truth it is not the same as *you* saying truth as we know truth. There is this difference between you and me.

And everybody else. And people to come and people who ever have been, there is this difference, between every single person, every single living breathing thing: everything, in one way or another, there is this. What is *this?* Patterns of thought, echoes of Tom. It is the striving itself, at the level he brings to it, that provides the profundity.

He was a master. And *we* need to be strong enough to say that of him, to honour him; to honour him for what he was and what he is. I doubt I could have said that to him. I doubt he would have coped with it. In the midst of his own self-belief, the essential self-belief without which his great work would not exist, in the midst of the faith he had in that, he had *such* humility.

Yes he was a master. But one of many. That is the strength of this tradition. From anywhere and everywhere, and from any historical period: take from it and give within it.

Tom is not only a major literary figure but of such power in the personal sense. His impact on people's lives is massive. For some of us the shock was heightened: we had been in touch with him in recent weeks, recent days even. We knew how poorly he had been but it was his indomitability; spiritual, intellectual. If Tom said he wasn't keeping great then we can make a guess about the reality, the sheer physical assault on the body he endured.

It's difficult for people to come to terms with what has happened. At the same time, he leaves a body of work that ensures his presence; the dialogue continues. One to one. That is Tom. Ye want to talk with Tom? Go to his work. How do you cope with the world? Do what Tom did. Don't hide. Do the best ye can.

If all human beings are unique the story of each person's life is unique. In answer to how many stories are there in the world we say as many as there are human beings; at least as many as there are human beings; more than there are human beings, as many as need be, and on we go.

Pick yerself up and get on with it. That is what Tom Leonard did, that is his lesson, that is Tom's lesson. What more can there be than one human being doing his best, doing her best, forever and ever. That is Tom Leonard.

Notes

What I Do is Write

1. This and other unattributed quotations are from the correspondence between myself and Mary Gray Hughes. Original letters and copies are in the National Library of Scotland and in the Mary Gray Hughes archive at the Southwestern Writers Collection, Texas State University, San Marcos, Texas, 78666-4604. This is a revised version of my introduction to her posthumous collection of stories, Cora's Seduction (Puckerbrush Press, 2002).

2. See Don Graham's Introduction (p1) to Uncovered Wagon by Hart Stilwell (Texas Monthly Press, 1985).

3. See Biographical Sketch at https://www.thewittliffcollections. txstate.edu/research/a-z/stilwell.html.

4. Ibid.

5. See Don Graham's Introduction (p1) to Uncovered Wagon by Hart Stilwell (Texas Monthly Press, 1985).

Why ain't the band playing?

1. The Anti-Apartheid movement was always active in Glasgow; see Brian Filling's essay 'Nelson Mandela and the Freedom of

Scotland's Cities' for information on the Scottish movement as a whole, included in The End of a Regime? (Mercat Press, 2002).

2. See https://www.sahistory.org.za/article/state-emergency-1985.

3. Published in Cencrastus magazine, autumn 1981.

4. In her essay found in Aspects of South African Literature, ed. C. Heywood (Heinemann, 1976).

5. Cencrastus (autumn 1981).

6. Tasks and Masks by Lewis Nkosi (Longman, 1981).

7. Ibid.

8. See South Africa: The Struggle for a Birthright by Mary Benson (Penguin African Library, 1966; reprinted 1985 by The International Defence and Aid Fund for Southern Africa).

9. The Struggle for South Africa: a Reference Guide to Movements, Organisations and Institutions by Rob Davies, Dan O'Meara and Sipho Diamini, vol. 2 (Zed Books, 1984).

10. In Tambo's essay 'Call to Revolution' included in Apartheid: A Collection of Writings on South African Racism, edited by Alex La Guma (Lawrence & Wishart, 1972).

11. Rob Davies, Dan O'Meara and Sipho Diamini, op. cit.

12. Nelson Mandela, quoted by Mary Benson, op. cit.

13. See Sechaba, July issue 1983, Harold Wolpe's article.

14. The accused were a microcosm of the country: six Africans, three whites (of whom one was quickly freed with charges withdrawn) and an Indian. See pp. 254–8 South Africa: The Struggle for a Birthright by Mary Benson. Only seven were sent to Robben Island, no white men.

15. See Ian Fullerton's article in Cencrastus, summer 1980.

16. The Hungarian critic Georg Lukács has written the seminal work on Kafka and 'modernism'.

17. In his Twelve African Writers Gerald Moore says differently. He believes La Guma's short stories are technically inferior to his novels, which I am disputing here.

18. Two of his poems can be read in the Race Today Review of February 1986.

19. See Edinburgh Review, number 69 (1985).

20. https://www.sahistory.org.za/article/african-national-congress-timeline-1990-1999.

21. Ibid.

22. Ibid.

23. Ibid.

In the Spirit of Harry McShane

1. I had yet to read his autobiography. This was dictated to Joan Smith over a period of two years. It is an exciting read, a thorough exposition of McShane's life and times: see No Mean Fighter, by Harry McShane and Joan Smith (Pluto Press, 1978).

2. See my Introduction to Born up a Close.

3. See her Philosophy & Revolution: from Hegel to Sartre and from Marx to Mao (Delta Publishing, 1973).

4. These ideas are central in John La Rose's perspective (see the memoir 'Liberation begins in the imagination').

5. For more in this connection see The Black Jacobins Reader, edited by Charles Forsdick and Christian Høgsbjerg.

6. The Scottish Contribution to Marxist Sociology by Ronald L.

Meek (reprinted from Democracy and the Labour Movement, Lawrence & Wishart, 1955). I have no doubt whatsoever that it came from Harry McShane.

7. See her Philosophy & Revolution: From Hegel to Sartre and from Marx to Mao (Delta Publishing 1973).

8. See https://imhojournal.org/articles/sixty-years-of-raya-dunayevs-kayas-marxism-and-freedom-then-and-now/.

9. Amongst Hugh's personal effects was her card of condolence following the tragic death of his youngest son.

10. Founder member of the SWP. See Paul Foot's Obituary from the Guardian: https://www.theguardian.com/news/2000/apr/11/guardian obituaries.paulfoot.

11. Michael Donnelly.

12. Hugh Savage and Leslie Forster among them.

13. Paul Foot, the campaigning journalist, was sharing the platform that evening.

14. The burial place of Karl Marx.

15. This quotation is taken from my essay 'Some Recent Attacks on the Rights of the People', from the collection Some Recent Attacks: Essays Cultural & Political.

16. The actor was Gary (Lewis) Stevenson, dressed as Napoleon. The day after this memorial event for Harry McShane an anti-poll tax rally took place in 1991. Gary performed a monologue of mine from the speakers' platform. When he came down from the platform he was arrested by the police. I advised the police that Gary only read 'the message', it was me wrote it. But they paid no heed and set about arresting the actor for swearing in public such as to

cause a Breach of the Peace. Eventually they released him without charge.

The courage Jeff had

1. This may have been The Baltimore Review.
2. See The Guardian, 26 January 1993.

June's Laugh

1. This was first published in Wasafiri Vol 34, No. 1, March 2019.
2. p68 Civil Wars by June Jordan (Beacon Press, 1981).
3. Ibid p17.
4. Ibid p18.
5. June died in 2002.

"Liberation begins in the Imagination"

1. This memoir begins from two earlier essays of mine: *The Caribbean Artists Movement (1966–72)* by Anne Walmsley (New Beacon Books, 1992) and *Say Hello to John La Rose* from the anthology Foundations of a Movement: A Tribute to John La Rose (New Beacon Books, 1991), edited by Roxy Harris and Sarah White.
2. Tom Leonard.
3. For an insight into the various commitments undertaken by John La Rose go to https://www.georgepadmoreinstitute.org/John%20 La%20Rose.
4. For further research and general information start at https://www. georgepadmoreinstitute.org.
5. Elaine and Tarlochan have now moved on.

6. UNITE nowadays.

7. See Linton Kwesi Johnson's obituary of John La Rose in the Guardian, 4 March 2006.

8. John La Rose explained this in the Variant interview 1994.

9. See my *Interview with John La Rose*. A reduced version of the interview was published in the spring of 1994 by Variant Magazine, edited by Malcolm Dickson. The fuller version was included in my And the Judges said . . . collection of essays.

10. Ibid.

11. See The Caribbean Artists Movement (1966–72) by Anne Walmsley (New Beacon Books, 1992) for this and following quotations, unless otherwise stated.

12. See also *Kaiso, Calypso Music*, David Rudder in conversation with John La Rose (New Beacon Books, 1990).

13. See note 57, Linton Kwesi Johnson's obituary of John La Rose in the Guardian, 4 March 2006.

14. I first heard my work so described in 1971–72 by an outraged member of an extra-mural class, in response to three short stories I handed in for class discussion.

15. See *Lonely Londoners and Dreaming Dundonians* by Grant Hill. For more on Selvon at Dundee: https://blog.dundee.ac.uk/one-dundee/lonely-londoners-and-dreaming-dundonians/.

16. Check it out at https://www.georgepadmoreinstitute.org/

An Artist lives in Scotland

1. This essay was written 2005, here revised.

2. This was Gordon Manning who eventually did move out on his own.

3. See Gray's introduction to the Five Scottish Artists Exhibition of 1986.

4. At Glasgow School of Art's Mackintosh Gallery.

Hugh Savage and the Workers City tradition

1. Leslie Forster's Rocking the Boat (Clydeside Press, 1997).

2. Sell and be Damned, The Glasgow Merrylee Housing Scandal of 1951 by Ned Donaldson and Leslie Forster (Clydeside Press, 1992).

3. Born Up a Close: Memoirs of a Brigton Boy by Hugh Savage (Argyll Publishing, 2006).

4. For more on James McLaren see Leslie Forster's Rocking the Boat (Clydeside Press, 1997).

The Voice of Amos Tutuola

1. This began as an obituary to Amos Tutuola who died in 1997 but has been revised thoroughly since then.

The writer John Mulligan

1. See the Obituary by Kevin Fagan, "John Mulligan: 1950–2005/ Author depicted Trauma of Vietnam war veterans" in SFGate, 23rd October, 2005.

"Rocking the Boat"

1. I spoke at Leslie's funeral, making direct quotations from his auto-biography, Rocking the Boat (Clydeside Press, 1991). I thought it gave a strong sense of Leslie himself; he was always opinionated, he never held back. Unless indicated all quotations are taken from it.

2. p77 One Great Vision . . . Memoirs of a Glasgow Worker, by Kenny McLachlan (published by the author, 1996).

3. For more information see Forster's Rocking the Boat, and Hugh Savage's Born up a Close.

4. Matt McGinn, musician, writer and activist.

5. Bill McCulloch was another Maryhill man, a writer and school-teacher.

6. The Singer Strike: Clydebank, 1911, by Glasgow Labour History Workshop (Clydebank District Library, 1989).

7. Three Days that Shook Edinburgh: Story of the Historic Scottish Hunger March by Harry McShane (AK Press, 1994).

8. All for the Cause: Willie Nairn 1856 - 1902, Stonebreaker, Philosopher, Marxist, written by Hugh Savage and Les Forster (Clydeside Press, 1991).

Oh sorry, wrong room

1. See https://www.austinchronicle.com/food/2003-07-04/166639/.

2. There is much to learn on James Sledd and his life: begin from Eloquent Dissent: The Writings of James Sledd, edited by Richard D. Freed (Boynton/Cook Publishers, 1996).

3. Noam Chomsky took one of his classes as a student. When I mentioned this to Jim he smiled, Yes, he sat in my class for a year.

4. Joe died in 2014 at the age of 86.

Tom

1. This is revised from the address I gave at Tom's funeral. He died on 21 December 2018.